Acclaim for

Chasing Hummingbirds

Discover the Empowering Force of Your Life Story

Chasing Hummingbirds is a celebration of self-reflection and growth. Montero Hernandez gently coaxes us to do a little "curious gazing" at our lives to learn from our personal stories, as she has learned from her own. She recounts a rich history of strong, flawed family members and the intergenerational trauma that shaped her youth. Her tales are compassionate and forgiving, ultimately revealing to the reader a roadmap for self-discovery. It's a beautifully written meditation on making meaning of life experiences and a perfect tonic for the chaos and uncertainty of the current moment.

Karen Oehme, Director, Student Resilience Project,
Florida State University

The process of personal transformation is fundamentally an act of resiliency. The accounts, realizations, and lessons we find in *Chasing Hummingbirds* show both the sensibility and courage that can reside in the human heart and mind. Montero Hernandez's brave and honest narrative shows the value of *curiously gazing* who we are, cultivating our ability to love, and authoring our lives deliberately. In this thoughtfully written and inspiring book, we find a caring and perceptive voice that reminds us to be brave, curious, loving, compassionate, and disciplined to find who we can become beyond the trauma or suffering of our past experiences. *Chasing Hummingbirds* is a well-structured invitation to re-imagine ourselves through the conscious and continual re-making of our life stories.

Gabriela Lilián González Flores,
Humanistic Gestalt Therapist

The essence of our being reverberates the echoes of our past. Montero Hernandez's *Chasing Hummingbirds* reminds us that these reflections carry a propensity for dissonance but also, if allowed through "curious gazing," for growth and resolution. Through personal stories, wit, and a dash of humor we find ourselves amidst Montero Hernandez's life, growing alongside her, identifying and empathizing with a plight whose cords resonate deeply. We see a heart yearning for growth despite setbacks and, if we allow it, it dawns on us that this struggle is a reflection of our own and her resolve and process become ours. May her growth mindset be yours—to find beauty in uncertainty and the ever-evolving narrative of your life's story.

David Hoyt, Computer Scientist and Father

In *Chasing Hummingbirds*, Montero Hernandez inspires and compels us to journey inward, to explore the complex and varied terrain of our own personal histories, to discover new understandings, and to integrate these new realizations in our approach to ourselves and others to bring about collective healing. Her deft use of the concept of curious gazing takes us on a journey through her own rich personal history and demonstrates how the examination of oneself and the collective memory of one's family can lead to new revelations that inspire more compassionate and enlightened ways to engage with ourselves and the people in our lives. *Chasing Hummingbirds* is a call to action. To look beyond. To go deeper. To unearth and examine the parts of ourselves and our histories that make us who we are. But most importantly, to recognize the magic unfolding in our lives each and every day.

Christine Cerven, PhD in Sociology and
Public Health Researcher

CHASING HUMMINGBIRDS

DISCOVER THE EMPOWERING
FORCE OF YOUR LIFE STORY

CHASING HUMMINGBIRDS

DISCOVER THE EMPOWERING FORCE OF YOUR LIFE STORY

VIRGINIA MONTERO HERNANDEZ

Published by Author Academy Elite

P.O. Box 43, Powel, OH 43035

www.AuthorAcademyElite.com

LCCN: 2021901307

ISBN: 978-1-64746-690-9 (Paperback)
ISBN: 978-1-64746-691-6 (Hardback)
ISBN: 978-1-64746-692-3 (E-book)

Available in hardcover, softcover, e-book, and audiobook.

Any Internet addresses (websites, blogs, etc.) printed in this book are offered as a resource. They are not intended in any way to be or imply an endorsement by Author Academy Elite, nor does Author Academy Elite vouch for the content of these sites for the life of this book.

Some names and identifying details have been changed to protect the privacy of individuals.

DEDICATION

To my intergenerational family whose pain and passion forged the chains of events that brought me here.

Papás y hermanos dedico este trabajo a ustedes porque la naturaleza infinita de su amor me inspira a seguir escribiendo una historia de vida plena.

To the women in my life whose endurance, devotion, and commitment to love allowed me to be hopeful. Your courage and intelligence inspired me to never give up.

To the men in my life whose assertiveness, authenticity, and audacity to live encouraged me to look further and aspire to greater things. Your tenderness and kindness equipped me to achieve.

To you, my reader, who have taken the challenge to look inward, to learn, and to expand the love that is in you.

Leyenda Alada

Colibrí, heraldo de la sincronía que orienta al universo
Tus plumas tornasol son sincretismo de sol, azul y jade
El rojo chinchilla de tu pecho se torna pincel en el cielo
Eres capricho de dioses y esperanza de hombres
Tu leyenda es el eco de memorias ancestrales

Colibrí de concertado vuelo, tu robusto latir inspira anhelos
La sedosa esencia de tus alas concilia milagro y don
Permíteme tocarte con un poema para no verte disolver en el viento
Quédate conmigo a escuchar la respiración de los árboles y el caracol
No dejes que te incinere en una mirada cautivada por la indiferencia,

Colibrí que conjuras danzas elocuentes y efímeras en el firmamento
Déjame sentirte mío cuando te imploro en un suspiro
Concédeme un instante en tu mirada y desvanece el caos que nos envuelve
Quiero ser tu aliada y que mi palabra te convierta en mensaje recurrente
Regálame el talento para evocarte en cada expresión de amor que
co-creamos hoy.

Winged Legend

Hummingbird, herald of the universe's synchronicity
Your iridescent feathers are a blend of sun, blue, and jade
The carmine red of your chest becomes a paintbrush in the sky
You are the whim of gods and men's hope
Your legend bears the echo of ancestral memories

Hummingbird of thoughtful flight, your robustly beating heart inspires will
The silky essence of your wings unites miracle and gift
Allow me to reach you with a poem so that the wind dissolves you not
Stay with me to hear the breathing of trees and snails
Do not let me burn you with a gaze infused by indifference

Hummingbird, you conjure eloquent and ephemeral dances in the firmament
Let me feel you are mine when I call upon you in a whisper
Allow me but an instant of your contemplation to elapse the chaos that surrounds us
Let me be your ally and transmute you in a never-ending message
Gift me the talent to recreate you through the love I give to the world.

CONTENTS

PART 2: REALIZING OUR CREATIVE ENERGY: THE LOVE THAT LIVES WITHIN US

PART 3: CO-CREATED STORIES: THE LOVE THAT CONNECTS US

FINAL WORDS

A NOTE TO THE READER

Once upon a Time a Hummingbird: The Story and Purpose of This Book

As you join me to walk this journey, I want to share a bit of the story behind the creation of this book. Through the personal accounts I will share with you, you will learn about who I am and the ways in which I learned to make sense of life and personal growth.

One of the premises of this book is that by sharing my story, you can find similarities in the experiences and challenges we have both found as part of our personal journeys. By reading my story, you can learn how to discover and explore specific episodes of your personal journey. In doing so you can achieve new awareness about your origins, who you are, and how you interact with others. This type of awareness is essential to achieve personal growth and empowerment. My intention is to help you navigate a process of self-discovery and self-actualization through the observation and re-interpretation of your personal story. Central to the examination of your own journey is the realization of the creative energy (love) that has made you who you are today.

I am a Mexican, professional, single woman in her late 30s living in a foreign country. My story is the story of a heart that lives in two places—Mexico and the United States—and speaks two languages. I chose this life, one that forces you to say many goodbyes, miss the people and place you love, and to seek constant change.

Since I was a child, I have loved hearing stories. My mother is a passionate storyteller. She loves narrating because she has intuitively realized the healing power of telling and retelling the stories that have made her. I learned to love stories because of her. She is also a story hunter. She often asks people what their stories are, and likes making sense of people through the stories they share with her. As an educator, she thought learning about her students' stories was the best way to take care of them. I grew up listening to my mom's stories and I continue to enjoy her storytelling.

What captivated me as a child became the core of my identity as an adult, too. In my personal and professional life, I see immense value in making sense of our own personal stories and taking the time to learn other people's life stories. As an educational researcher, I understand the value stories have in the formation of our lives and identities. We use narratives to interpret ourselves retrospectively, to understand our present lives, and to define who we expect to become. The words and expressions we choose to describe each event of our life—every turning point and experience—shape who we are. We construct ourselves through the narratives we tell to ourselves and others.

I write this book to remind us of the value of personal stories and the healing power that exists in the act of telling and retelling our personal stories from a place of higher awareness and compassion toward ourselves and others. This book is not intended as an act of self-aggrandizement. Rather, it attempts to show vulnerability and humility as conditions to learn and to inspire others to do the same. Primarily, I re-tell my personal stories to show the healing power of re-interpreting our lives from a place of empowerment in which we view ourselves as capable to overcome struggle, to expand the interpretations of our actions (to reframe them), and to re-write our lives.

It is important to clarify, the retelling of my personal stories and the re-interpretation that comes along with it did not occur during the year in which I wrote this book. Instead, the realization of the value of my stories, my reflection on each one of them, and the possibility of re-interpretation all took place gradually over the last decade.

Personal growth is a process that takes time and requires continual attention. It is the constant observation, appreciation, analysis, and reframing of our stories that helps us become a better version of ourselves. This book is my effort to capture that process and offer you insights that can help guide you during your own process.

The approach that informs this book is based on narrative therapy, a form of therapy that acknowledges humans' storytelling abilities as a pathway to encourage personal healing and growth.[1] This therapeutic practice acknowledges that individuals use stories to make sense of themselves and the events of their lives. However, when we tell our stories, we always tell them from a particular standpoint. Sometimes, we tell our stories from a place of frustration, fear, hesitation, or sadness. Other times, we tell our stories from a place of trust, joy, confidence, and satisfaction. Usually the stories that incorporate a positive mindset allow us to keep our lives moving forward, whereas the stories we tell ourselves and others from a negative mindset are more likely to keep us stuck.

The purpose of narrative therapy is to help a person examine his or her narratives so they can reframe negative meanings associated to his or her personal stories. Engaging in personal storytelling from a standpoint of confidence, trust, and empowerment can help the person to move their life forward.

Empowered storytelling is based on the idea that we can reframe the ways in which we remember and make sense of the events of our lives. In doing so, we position ourselves as active spectators and authors of our lives rather than victims or passive observers.

Narrative therapy reminds us of the creative capacity we have to interpret and re-interpret the stories of our lives. Each one of us can engage in narrative therapy when we make a conscious effort to retell our stories from a standpoint that makes us feel more confident and empowered to author our lives. When we are intentional in observing and narrating the beauty, the lessons, the growth, and the love that lies underneath each one of the personal stories we tell, we can then stimulate personal growth in ourselves.

The writing of this book represents my own effort to engage in a form of narrative therapy. Additionally, by telling and examining my personal story, I aim to help others learn how to make sense of their own stories and reframe them from a position of empowerment. My goal is to help you realize your stories can be a great source for self-actualization. I invite you to pay attention to, reflect on, and reframe (from an empowering perspective) the stories that have shaped your life's journey up to this day.

I have realized people learn best when they can see the real human being behind the teacher, and when there are concrete examples to learn from. I hope you—whether you are a man or a woman—can relate to the stories I share with you here. Many of us share similar struggles and hopes as we build our lives. It is this conviction that encouraged me to take the risk of disclosing my personal life, even some of the more vulnerable aspects of my journey.

Learning about the story of a person like me—a professional single woman—can be relevant within a contemporary world where more and more professional women enter the job market and dare to balance a private and public life in a rapidly changing and complex society. I know many professional women in our society may be facing challenges and dilemmas similar to the ones I describe here. By sharing my story, I also aim to shed light on the various challenges and struggles that many of us endure in silence and shame, simply because we don't realize many other people experience similar forms of distress.

My story can also be important for those men who are curious and intrigued about understanding the challenges that contemporary women experience in this modern world. Although my life story does not represent all types of professional women out there, I am sure it can offer some clues about the type of lives such women seek to create. It is my sincere desire that my personal accounts and the ways in which I have made sense of them can be useful for both men and women.

Most importantly, I want to show we have the ability and authority to narrate our stories in unique and empowered ways. In the interpretation and retelling of my life story, you will find a mix of magic and realism in the ways I make sense of everything. That is how I see and construct life. I consider myself a rational woman. I am a social scientist as part of my formal education and profession. My life, however, would not be complete without the pieces of magic and mysticism that help me expand the meaning of my personal journey.

My story, my message, and my advice come from two worlds: a world in which rationality gives us logical principles to order our reality, and another world made of faith, intuition, and imagination. The latter brings alternative and complementary ways to understand my existence in this non-rational reality. In orchestrating my life, I rely on reason as much as faith.

While writing this book, I had three specific goals in mind:

Firstly, I want to encourage my readers to engage in a process of self-growth by looking inwards and realizing the value of the stories that shape their personal journey.

Secondly, I aim to inspire you to engage in a compassionate yet critical examination of your personal stories to realize the inner strengths and personal resources you can use to succeed.

Thirdly, I hope the message of this book will bring us closer to one another by learning about each other's stories and understanding the love (creative energy) that connects us and brought us here today. It is my hope our mutual and compassionate understanding of each other as members of a society can lead us to co-creating meaningful stories together.

Now you understand the purpose of this book, let me tell you about how its title was born. The title of this book came as a whisper to my heart. One day, without too much warning, I heard the title, *Chasing Hummingbirds*, in my head and it stayed with me like a persistent knocking at the door, asking me to let it in. Hummingbirds were both the messenger and the message itself.

Chasing hummingbirds is a metaphor I decided to use to refer to the subtle action of paying attention to these beautiful miracles *flying around* us and *through* us. Chasing a hummingbird with our eyes to admire their splendor in the air is a mindful act. Following the flight of a hummingbird—chasing them with our eyes—often demands being still and carefully observant to allow us to capture the color, movement, sounds, and unique nature of this amazing bird. The attentive and curious eye will see the exquisiteness of these birds. Every time I see a hummingbird flying around where I am, they remind me that there is amazing beauty in our life if we dare to look closer and deeper.

Similarly, understanding and honoring the miracles within our own existence and stories require an attentive and curious disposition. We cannot truly acknowledge and value the uniqueness of our roots, the source of our strength, or the force of the love that created us without taking a mindful and reflective position toward our personal journeys.

My enchantment with hummingbirds is not by chance. As a child, every time my mom and I saw a hummingbird, she would exclaim, *"Mira un colibrí, mira que bonito, ya viste que rapido vuela? Los colibris simbolizan el amor. Asi que tendrás buena suerte.* Look at that hummingbird; look how beautiful it is and how fast it flies. Hummingbirds symbolize love. This means you will have luck in love."

For my mom, hummingbirds are a celebration in the sky; they are heralds of good fortune. Although she didn't realize it then, my mom gave me a piece of magic from her world and in doing so, she shaped my world too. As the hummingbirds became part of my magic world, I started thinking of them as creatures that bring together science and spirituality. Over the years, I learned both mystical and scientific facts about them.

As a statement of biological perfection, hummingbirds challenge the logics of nature by having a heart rate of 1,200 beats per minute and the ability to go up, down, sideways, backwards, and even upside down. The flying pattern of their wings shape the number eight—the symbol of infinity. The proportion of muscles in their chest and the types of bones in their wings create their ability to turn flying into poetry. Because of their fast metabolism, they can consume up to double their body weight in a day.

While seemingly tiny and fragile birds at first glance, hummingbirds are assertive and fearless when it comes to defending their territory. They migrate over large territories, or travel alone for up to 500 miles at a time. Hummingbirds also have a powerful brain that represents 4.2% of their body weight, making them unique within the wild bird group. Hummingbirds have an amazing capacity to remember all the flowers they have visited to eat their nectar. They memorize the places they have been to create effective flying trajectories.

Hummingbirds are primarily found in the American continent. Cuba is the home of the tiniest hummingbird species, the bee hummingbird. The amazing hummingbird is a nectarivore—the main ingredient of its diet is nectar, the essence of flowers. By taking the nectar, hummingbirds help spread pollen, making flowering and fruit-bearing plants possible. As a result, hummingbirds are also creators of beauty.

As a statement of spirituality, hummingbirds are carriers of symbolic messages. Due to their unique composition and place in the bird kingdom, some of the meanings attached to them are adaptability, resiliency, lightness of being, enjoyment of life, independence, and love. It turns out my mom wasn't wrong—hummingbirds are symbols of love. One of the Mayan legends I learned about recounts that when the gods created the world, they gave a mission to each living and non-living thing in the universe. When they'd finished the creation, however, they realized they hadn't created anything that could deliver their desires and thoughts to the humans. So, they took a jade stone, drew an arrow in it, and then they breathed life into it. As they did so, the arrow became alive and started to fly. That was how the hummingbird was created to carry messages from the gods to the humans on earth.

The hummingbird is so light it is able to approach the most delicate flowers without moving a single petal. Their colorful and shiny feathers refract the light of the sun in multicolor shades. The legend tells that once men on earth saw the amazing colors of the tiny birds' bodies, they tried to capture them to use their feathers to decorate their clothes. The action of men upset the gods, who prohibited men to hunt the birds.

As messengers of the gods, hummingbirds were also given the duty of carrying thoughts or feelings between humans. The Mayans said seeing a hummingbird was a signal of someone sending joyful thoughts and love. Similar to this Mayan story, other myths note that angels chose hummingbirds to deliver their messages to humans. Hummingbirds are a reminder of the existence of magic in a logical world.

This book is an invitation for you to *chase the hummingbirds*—the splendor and beauty—hidden in the stories of your life. As you reflect upon your own existence, I encourage you to discover the love and wealth embedded in each episode of your life.

As you prepare to start reading the first chapter, I would like to remind you I write for you with a humble heart. My voice does not come from a place of achieved perfection but rather constant remaking and self-forgiveness. I write from a place of courage in which I try to accept that we are constantly learning to improve ourselves. I also write from a place of gratitude and service. I thank you for your willingness to open your heart to my message and for trying to be a better person through the experiences that make up your every day. This world needs brave people like you, willing to look inwards and invest the work that is required to improve.

In each section of this book, I will share several of my personal stories. By presenting my interpretation of each of these stories, I want to help you realize the ways in which we can engage in the *observation, analysis,* and *reframing* of our stories so we can learn and grow. There is healing power in the possibility to reframe (give a different meaning to) our stories in ways that help move our lives forward.

The stories and knowledge shared in this book can be equally applicable for women and men because I tried to identify themes relevant for everyone: fear, self-doubt, low self-esteem, personal-work dilemmas, dating, loneliness, family dynamics, and so on. While my experiences are not a representation of what all women or men in the world think and feel, I believe they mirror many of the challenges and desires other women (and men) live as part of their journey.

This book is also an invitation for men and women to come together and learn to share their personal stories with each other as a way to be compassionate and grow together. In my personal website (www.creativeselfdesign.com), you can find and download a chart with specific questions that will help you dive into the story of your life, reflect on the various stories that shape your personal journey, and re-interpret the experiences you have had. The use of this chart can guide you in the discovery of the love embedded in your life and the personal resources you have to grow and expand who you are.

PART 1

APPRECIATING THE LOVE THAT CREATED US

NOTES FROM A HUMMINGBIRD

*Curious gazing is a subtle and persistent act of conscious exam-
ination and (re)interpretation of our stories; each narrative of
empowerment we create is a step closer to a place of personal
contentment.*

One essential disposition or attitude toward one's existence
is what I have defined *curious gazing*. This life disposition
allows us to explore our life stories—those that have already
passed, those we are authoring right now, and those we have
the potential to create—and learn about ourselves.

Curious gazing is essential to chasing the hummingbirds
in your life stories. This observant disposition is important
to achieve two critical conditions: social and self-awareness.
Social awareness refers to one's ability to understand the
position(s) and role(s) we occupy in society. This type of
awareness involves understanding our family roots, how we
are connected to one another, the type of power we have access
to, the resources we have attained (or not), the culture we
embrace, and the traditions and values we hold dear to our
hearts. Self-awareness includes the ability to understand our
inner life and the realization of the unique ways in which we
think, feel, and behave toward ourselves and others.

Self- and social awareness are interconnected; the more we know about our social position the more we can understand how and why we have developed our psyche, personal attributes, and behaviors. At the same time, the more we learn about the type of self we have become, the more we understand how we arrived at the place we occupy in society.

Self- and social awareness are abilities we can develop through our life's journey. Life experiences and a deliberate desire to learn from those experiences can help us become more aware of our social place and our inner life. Curious gazing can make us aware of our origins, place in society, and intrapersonal life. An important aspect of self- and social awareness is understanding where we come from and how our story began.

Curious gazing can lead us to uncover *love as a vital creative energy* that has shaped our lives since the very first moment we were conceived. When I talk of love, I am not referring exclusively to romantic love or filial love. I understand love as a vital energy that moves us toward the creation of life in all its dimensions through art, knowledge, hope, joy, education, and learning. Love is the energy that moves us to wake up every day, overcome difficulties, become better individuals, aspire for greatness, become resilient, discover new knowledge, and serve others (animals, plants, or humans).

Curious gazing is based on our ability to self-reflect upon our life story and the stories connected to us. It can become a life disposition accessible to us when we pause our busy schedules and take some time to observe and reflect upon our past and present life. Further, it can lead us to uncover the miraculous set of events and people who conspired time after time to create who we are today and the opportunities that have unfolded for us.

Curious gazing can enable us to expand our being through patient observation, critical questioning, and continual reflection on who we are, where we come from, and where we are today. Curiosity is essential in our gazing; curiosity implies a desire to discover and learn, to be amazed, and to approach our existence with excitement.

I've established the disposition of curious gazing is vitally important to gain social and self-awareness. An enriched understanding of where we come from, where we are today, and who we are is crucial to discover the love that created us and sustains our life. In the next chapters, I will share with you how to develop curious gazing as a life disposition that can help you make sense of your life stories and the place where you are today.

1

CURIOUS GAZING: DISCOVERING AND CULTIVATING IT AS A LIFE DISPOSITION

The contemporary world can be a distracting place when we try to understand who we are and what life pathway we want to choose. From the day we are born to the day we say goodbye, both men and women hear competing messages about who they should be or what they should pursue in life. Whether intentionally or not, both women and men are constantly focused on the social mandates to follow. Sometimes, when we pay too much attention to the external social mandates, we tend to forget our internal voice, our intuitive knowledge, our inner spiritual self. When we become excessively focused on the outside world, we can delay the development of heightened self-awareness.

The modern woman and man are expected to be in motion all the time. Being chronically busy seems to be the new recipe for personal success, even if being busy sometimes leaves limited time to be in touch with our inner selves. It can feel counterintuitive to slow down when one has to hurry up to be the successful modern person one seeks to become persistently. However, it takes internal silence and focused intention to discover ourselves in the midst of the noise of society. The risk of not making a pause and engaging in curious gazing is that we can overlook the essence of who we are, the context we live in, and the stories of the people around us.

Finding that place of silence and attention in a distracting world doesn't come easy for many of us because we weren't taught from an early age to see ourselves as objects of contemplation, learning, and respect. We simply don't see ourselves as beautiful, intricate, and worthy fields for exploration. My life journey has taught me it's important to gaze curiously at ourselves, those around us, and the world we inhabit.

Curious gazing emerges as an opportunity to reconnect with ourselves and to understand our reality. It is also closely connected to mindfulness (being contemplative of the present moment) because it asks us to pause for a moment and appreciate what life is offering us.

Curious gazing starts with a disposition to be contemplative; however, it goes beyond that. It invites us to pose critical questions about our lives. Why am I here? How did I get here? What is the story of my life? What is the meaning of that story? What do I need to change? How did I become who I am today? Why did I feel this way? Why did I react in that way? What do I really want? What does that person bring to my life? What should I be grateful for? Curious gazing fosters greater emotional maturity; it enables us not only to contemplate and make sense of ourselves but also to develop sensibility toward and compassion for those around us.

Everyone can activate the ability to gaze their lives curiously; however, to do that, we need to become aware of the use and benefits of engaging in curious gazing as an everyday practice. As you read my story, I would encourage you to identify points of commonality with your own life trajectory. In doing so, you can start identifying how you've already engaged in curious gazing and how you can enhance that disposition even more. My disposition for curious gazing was instilled as a result of my life experiences and my intellectual curiosity. Practicing curious gazing helped me pay attention to my life and achieve personal growth. Most importantly, my curious gazing helped me make sense of the love that has brought me to the place where I am today.

When I was in my early twenties, I started to develop a passion for observing how people become who they are and what type of conditions or events shape who they are. This passionate curiosity was not incidental but rather due to the way in which my parents molded the early years of my life.

As it happened, I went to school from the age of 3. My parents worked as school teachers. They didn't want to leave me in daycare and they didn't have anyone who could help them to babysit. Therefore, my mom received permission to bring me to classes with her every day. She asked me to be well-behaved while she was teaching, and to do the lessons she'd prepared for me. She recalls I enjoyed being in class with her, observing the students, playing by myself, and falling asleep when I felt like doing so. Because of this situation, I spent a great deal of time with my mom during the first years of my life. She talked a lot to me; she liked telling me stories, giving me advice, answering my questions, and so on.

My mother is a very observant woman. She pays attention to everything, everywhere, and everyone. As a child and student, my mom instilled in me and my two brothers the importance of being observant, constantly advising us to pay attention to the things around us. Particularly when we were at home doing chores, she insisted emphatically, "*Pon atención a todo lo que haces, observa qué falta, observa en qué puedes ayudar, no te enfoques solo en tu metro cuadrado. Siempre piensa qué más puedes hacer.* Pay attention to everything you do; be observant about what is lacking; observe what you can do to help; do not be narrow minded; don't focus exclusively on the square meter in which you are standing; always think what else you can do." Even at this point in my life, she tells me, "*Virginia tienes que poner atencion, observa siempre a tu alrededor.* Virginia, you must be attentive; observe everything that occurs around you."

My mom had to develop that disposition as part of her own journey. She lost her mom as a result of domestic violence when she was eleven years old. Shortly after her mom died, my mom and her siblings were taken to an orphanage called *Casa Hogar Nuestros Pequeños Hermanos*[2] where they would live the next decades of their lives and where she would meet my father. For her, being attentive to everything around her was a matter of self-preservation in a context where she lived with other children and adults. Consequently, she wanted to make sure I was always aware of where I was, who I was, and who other people were.

The instruction to be observant didn't only come from my mom. My father had his own way of evoking my attention and curiosity. He would tell me to be observant of nature and its miracles. While my mother advised me to be observant of people and events taking place, my father advised me to be observant of the sky, the plants, and the animals. He has always been captivated by the greatness of nature and is as equally mesmerized by the smallest insect as he is by the cloudy sky or a storm.

My father's appreciation of nature came from his father who was a farmer and a healer using natural remedies to cure people. My grandfather, Margarito, whom I never met, was a man whose life was connected to nature. Although my father lost his father when he was only 8 years old due to a strange illness Margarito couldn't overcome, his origins were irrevocably tied to agriculture and raising animals.

My father's mother had already died during childbirth, so on the death of his father, he was put in the same orphanage where my mother would eventually arrive. There, he spent his free time hiking around the hacienda where they lived. My father recalls with infinite joy his adventures eating fruit from trees, cactus leaves, corn, and even small birds he and his friends caught sometimes. My father taught me to honor and respect nature through my careful observation of its miraculous existence. My father reminded me every small creature in this world is worthy of admiration and respect.

I lived my childhood and teenage years with a mandate to be observant and appreciative of the things, people, and nature in the world around me. That disposition expanded through my formal education and my career as a professor.

Inspired by my mom's advice, I enrolled in a BA in educational planning and assessment in a public Mexican state university. After I graduated, Omar, one of my mentors, advised me to continue my education. With Omar's guidance, I was granted a fellowship to study a graduate program abroad. I enrolled at the University of California as a doctoral student and became an educational researcher.

Once I finished my graduate education, I went back to my own country to work as a professor for the next four years. During the last two years of my time in Mexico, I started applying for jobs in the United States and was eventually hired as a university professor in Central California. The experience of becoming an international professional and bicultural person would push me to pay greater attention to the things around me and to my own existence in particular.

Living in a foreign country and having to use a different language can be a challenging, stressful, and scary experience. Being a foreigner is a life event that asks for braveness of the heart. It requires a lot of flexibility and adaptability. During the almost twelve years I've lived in the United States, I can say without hesitation being observant and having an authentic desire to learn about everything and anything around me was crucial to building a life. One has to approach a foreign land with an authentic intention to make sense of others, to connect with them, and to learn about their cultural rules and ways. Although most of my daily life while growing up fostered the habit of being observant, it was the act of living abroad that accelerated both my development and awareness of curious gazing as a life disposition.

When I left home to live in a different country, I had to refine my observant disposition and curiosity. When one lives independently, one has to pay attention to everything and everyone around, not only as a self-preservation predisposition but also as a way to grasp the beauty and complexity that shape the reality we live in. Additionally, living in a foreign country, away from one's family and usual environment, creates experiences of isolation that are intermittently suspended by interaction with others. However, it is in those spaces of solitude that the development of curious gazing becomes possible.

In the silence of an independent life in a foreign place, it became unavoidable to gaze at myself and those around me. Away from my family, with no responsibilities other than looking after myself, I recognized myself as a source of learning. With a new approach to reconnecting with my early observant abilities, my journey into self-observation, self-understanding, and self-growth began.

Curious gazing can help us understand ourselves in a more authentic and honest way. The power of curious self-gazing comes from one's ability to contemplate oneself as a field for exploration and inquiry, a new land that can offer infinite opportunities for learning. It includes compassion as much as critical self-reflection; it includes humility as much as confidence to follow one's desire to learn; it includes patience to understand oneself as much as persistence to believe in one's strength and self-efficacy.

Core to curious gazing is the act of asking oneself compassionate yet critical questions. Critical self-questioning is only possible from a position of humility—the acknowledgment that we don't know everything about life or ourselves. Humble and compassionate curious gazing will ask questions that help us to expand our self-understanding.

As importantly, this self-questioning cannot come from a position of judgment or hyper self-criticism, which can resemble something like this: Why am I reacting in such a stupid way? What is wrong with me? How can I still be feeling like this after so many days? Why am I so silly? Why haven't I improved by now, am I stupid? Why do I keep making the same mistake?

The practice of curious gazing helped me become aware of myself and the people with whom I interacted. Particularly, I wanted to understand why I seemed to experience a constant and unshakable feeling of sadness and loneliness. Although the cultural shock of living alone in a foreign country could be enough explanation to make sense of the void I felt, I wanted to understand more about myself and my emotions. I wanted to understand why I was feeling sad when I had the privilege of studying and then working abroad. I wanted to stop feeling guilty about not being appreciative enough for this life-changing opportunity. I felt it was wrong to be sad when I had so much to be grateful for: great learning opportunities, a great job, food and a place to live, a supportive family (even though they were a country away), caring friends (in both countries), and loyal, loving dogs.

Over the years, curious gazing has become the tool that helped me make sense of myself and the place where I am today. Turning to curious gazing resulted from intuition, inner wisdom, or something I may have learned before. When I started viewing myself as an object for inquiry, something important occurred. I realized to understand myself deeper and more fully, I had to turn my gaze toward other scenarios. I needed to understand where I was standing at that point in time from a social and cultural point of view. I also needed to understand where I came from, what my historical and psychological roots were.

As my practice of curious gazing started to expand, new horizons for gazing emerged: the society where I live and work, my intergenerational family (my ancestors), and the significant others who came into my life.

Curious gazing is not restricted to understanding our inner life; it requires us to see beyond our individual existence and acknowledge we are part of a system and a web of interconnected stories that started before we were born. Curious gazing nurtures both self- and social awareness.

2

GAZING THE COLLECTIVE SELF: THE STRESS SURROUNDING MEN AND WOMEN

Curious gazing aims to develop our social awareness—our ability to observe, question, and make sense of the world and the position we occupy in it. Gaining social awareness is crucial to contextualize our existence. It involves understanding two critical aspects: the ways in which society has left its mark on us, and the ways in which we leave our mark on society.

The ideologies we are surrounded by, the cultural practices we preserve in our families, the language we use, and the traditions we celebrate shape the ways in which we decide to make sense of life. Simultaneously, every single action we do, either actively or passively, contributes to create the institutions and regulations we live by. Being aware of the relationship between our individual and collective selves is fundamental to making decisions from a place of consciousness.

The collective self, which I call society, is made up of the intersection of individual and collective stories. We come together as individuals to create organizations, implement altruistic causes, initiate wars, lead rescue missions, preserve nature, destruct natural habitats, celebrate accomplishments, create tensions, develop cures and healing formulas, and design material innovations. The rhythm and direction of human creation are vast. It is in this never-ending occurrence of events that our lives and stories are co-constructed.

One of the collective experiences we sense as members of this social world is the increasing level of stress permeating our daily routines.[3] Both stress and anxiety have become serious issues of contemporary life. Chronic exhaustion, emotional fatigue, migraines, burn out syndrome, and other related conditions have become common manifestations in people's bodies and minds. My own personal story is not free from the impact of anxiety and stress. However, I have learned curious gazing can be an ally in our attempts to understand where our stress comes from or how we can learn to liberate ourselves from it.

We, as a society, live under constant pressure to succeed professionally, romantically, and financially. Through my curious gazing, I have realized these constant pressures impact the ways in which men, women, and families see and treat themselves. In my work as an educational researcher, I see and experience some detrimental effects of anxiety and stress in women. As a relatively new member of the professional world, I notice women often feel divided between their desire to excel professionally and to express their caring, feminine self.

As part of my personal and professional experience, I had the opportunity to talk to several women who worked as professors.[4] All of them reported psychological distress in the form of guilt, impostor syndrome, or frustration. Some of them, particularly those who were married, reported feeling mediocre as mothers, as professionals, and as wives. They felt excessive pressure to excel in all the different dimensions of their lives. Their perceived failure to successfully meet social expectations of their roles made them feel negative about themselves and to manifest their psychological distress in different physical ways: digestive issues, bumps in their body, muscle tension, chronic fatigue, insomnia, and so on.

Single professional women—like me—don't have an easier scenario. While we may not have the pressures of having a husband or children, we still have families (parents, siblings, extended family) along with the related obligations and concerns. While married professional women have a busy life to worry about, single professional women have spaces of solitude that we have to learn how to inhabit, particularly in a world that glorifies couples. As I paid attention to the lives of many other women with pathways similar to mine, I found the mental health issues I experienced were part of a collectively shared wound.

My curious gazing didn't stop with my realizations about professional women; I wanted to understand how men were doing in the contemporary world as well. It turns out that it's not very different for men. In this demanding world, men also have high expectations and roles they are trying to fulfill every day.

While men have historically been in the professional world longer than women, they experience other types of challenges. For example, they are encouraged, without too much guidance, to reconfigure traditional views of masculinity while creating more caring and softer male behaviors. Similar to women, men have to navigate contradictory mandates: they are expected to be both physically strong and delicate, in control and yet emotionally open and vulnerable, sexually assertive and loyal, job-oriented and domestically available, ambitious yet content with simple pleasures.

As part of my personal and professional life, I have learned about the stories of young and mature men. In their stories, I hear and see the ways in which some men respond to traditional values and practices of hyper-masculinity: the unquestioned compliance with emotional restrain and avoidance, the need to show aggression and violence as a way to demand social respect and status, the rejection of their feminine self so as not to have their masculinity questioned, and the expression of hyper-sexualized behavior and objectification of women as a sign of dominance. Men also live in a constant state of stress and anxiety that comes from the cultural messages and expectations imposed upon them every day.

My gazing of the collective self showed me there is a shared sense of psychological distress that both men and women experience as part of their everyday lives. Both men and women dare to exist and become someone in the midst of confusing and contradictory demands. While there is nothing wrong with having women connecting and embracing their masculine attributes, and having men connecting with their feminine side, I have the sensation that society has not yet created safe conditions and guidance that enable women and men to analyze, understand, and discriminate contradictory social mandates. At the end of the day, we are left with a series of social expectations and prescriptions that often don't translate into everyday practical ways that allow individuals to be happier and interact in healthier ways. As a result, finding the appropriate mix of our feminine and masculine selves is a personal battle.

While my curious gaze has taken me to reflect on gender dynamics and gender roles in society, I also realize the complexity of our social world is not exhausted in a discussion of the different ways in which men and women experience life. In our society, issues of race and social class are also arenas for deeper reflection. Particularly in a multicultural, immigrant-based country like the United States, differences in culture, ethnicity, and socioeconomic status can create multiple challenges for men and women. Therefore, it is a personal responsibility to use our curious gazing to gain social awareness of the myriad of experiences shaping the stories of people close to us and around the world.

The realization that society can be a demanding and confusing place where men and women struggle to find themselves helped me understand I wasn't alone in my struggle to find myself. I recognized part of my psychological distress came from the complexity of living in a contemporary world where individualism and collectivism are presented to society as equally desirable and threatening ways of living. My realizations helped me to see myself with more compassion and to show more patience toward myself when feeling psychological distress, particularly when such distress was associated with the process of creating a new life in a foreign country.

While my curious gazing helped me realize the challenges and tensions residing in the collective self in which we live, I also realized people can be compassionate toward each other's struggles. In the midst of the social complexity, I was able to appreciate that individuals, groups, and organizations come together to address the issues affecting our lives. Awareness about mental health issues, acceptance of cultural differences and skin color, tolerance of a diversified understanding, and an embrace of sexuality continue to be contested terrains. More and more advocates, however, continue to fight to promote acceptance, respect, and solidarity.

The collective self in which we co-create our lives is capable of offering not only tensions and demands but also expressions of compassion and love toward humankind. It is through that sense of hope that it becomes possible for us to overcome our everyday tensions and demands.

3

GAZING OUR INTERGENERATIONAL FAMILIES: THE ROOTS OF WHO WE ARE

While the curious gazing of the cultural and social world around us can help us partially understand the sources of our distress, not all the answers are there. One needs to carefully learn and observe one's family tree and the underlying intergenerational trauma and resiliency.

On my route toward self-understanding, my curious self-gazing led me to pose more questions about my personal story and the stories before I was born. I wanted to understand, how did my parents meet? When and how did they decide to have children? How was their childhood? What have they learned about being parents? Why was I given my first name? What has been painful across the generations?

Once, when I was in my early 20s, I was listening to a radio station my mom enjoyed. I heard about a systemic therapy that helps individuals understand their family's intergenerational trauma and the ways in which this trauma is passed from one generation to the next until a member of the family becomes aware of the patterns of pain and exclusion and chooses to break that vicious cycle. Known as Family Constellations,[5] this therapy has become a well-known approach to help individuals unravel unconscious, destructive, and repetitive family patterns, and unconscious harmful agreements that family members pass down through the generations as a way of maintaining a sense of belonging to the family group.

The founder of this therapeutic method was Bert Hellinger, a German Catholic man who had studied theology, pedagogy, and psychology. He developed the series of principles forming the basis of his therapeutic methodology by observing family communities during his missionary work in South Africa over several decades. His work and teachings have guided many initiatives to understand, heal, and expand family dynamics toward healthier states of being. While some people find Hellinger's approach lacking in scientific rigor, Family Constellations is still a widely accepted method among some therapists, spiritual healers, and other thinkers.

During the last eight years of my life, I became more intensely attracted to this therapeutic approach which guided me to understand the story of my ancestors and the traumas that affected my parents and ultimately touched my brothers and me. One important condition that allowed me to make sense of my intergenerational roots was my mom's devoted telling and retelling of her past. My mother is a great story teller and has an amazing memory. She enjoyed telling and retelling family stories, even if she relived part of the pain in every account. I also feel her storytelling helped me develop a more compassionate view of her as a human being, beyond her role as my mother.

Additionally, for me, it was difficult to ignore the weight of my family's past when I'd inherited my given first name from my maternal grandmother. One of the family traditions my mom honored was the naming of the first born after the grandparents. My mother's mom was named Virginia and with her death it became my mission to carry her name.

Truth be told, I always struggled to feel entirely comfortable with my first name—Virginia sounded far too serious and formal to me. Fortunately, it became more acceptable because everyone in my family called me Vicky, which in Mexico is a common nickname for Virginia. Only occasionally—when my mom or dad was mad—would they call me Virginia, which didn't help much to establish a positive connection with my name. Sometimes, my inherited name made me feel as though I was caught between myself and someone I'd never met.

Virginia, my grandmother, died in her early 30s as a result of domestic violence, leaving behind four children: two boys and two girls. My grandmother didn't have an easy life, growing up with her mom and an absent father. My great grandmother had to raise six children by herself. She worked tirelessly to be able to feed and dress her children, often having to leave them unattended at home for many long hours. Probably as part of an emotionally deprived childhood, my grandmother developed self-esteem issues that later manifested difficulties to walk out on an abusive relationship. Tragically, this meant my mother and her siblings repeatedly witnessed domestic violence.

My mom and her family lived in Mexico City. She and her sister were forced into premature adulthood, learning to navigate the city on their own and take care of their brothers and family duties at a very early age. For my mom, seeing her mother's suffering was a severely traumatic experience that left deep scars. With the best of her abilities and a resilient spirit, my mom found the strength to live and to build a family of her own. While I see in my mother the strength of a persistent woman, I still—even now—recognize in her eyes the scars of her past and her resilient spirit's effort to forget what hurt her as a vulnerable child.

A short time after my grandmother died, my mother and her siblings were taken to *Casa Hogar Nuestros Pequeños Hermanos (NPH)*, a charitable organization that has provided a home for thousands of orphans and abandoned children since 1954. The organization was founded by William B. Wasson, an American priest from Arizona, who opened the orphanage in Cuernavaca, Morelos in Mexico.

At NPH, my mom shouldered the responsibility and pressure to look after her two little brothers. She describes her life there as a mix of both enjoyable and sad experiences. She struggled to feel loved and be seen in the midst of a crowd of children who shared similar or even more dramatic past lives. While my mom enjoyed the opportunity to grow up surrounded by other children who would become lifetime friends, she always missed her mother.

The story of how my father lost his parents is also sad but he didn't witness domestic violence as a child. My paternal grandparents lived with their children—my father and his brother—in a rural town. My grandfather, Margarito, was a farmer and a healer with psychic abilities. He enjoyed working in the fields and raising animals. My father tells of how his father was a lover of nature and the simple ways of life. My father would join him in his field work and learned to love nature as much as his father.

My father's mother was a stay-at-home housewife. She died while giving birth to her third child, a baby girl. My grandfather died a year later of an intense stomach pain that he could not overcome. While my father's family attribute his death to witchcraft, the real cause of his death remains an unsolved mystery.

My father doesn't remember his childhood as a traumatic period of his life. While he does remember the pain and suffering of losing his parents, he also remembers the happiness of life in the country and his close contact with nature. My father was eight years old when he entered NPH. From that point on, he and his four-year-old brother, Roberto, started building new life memories. For my father, life in the orphanage allowed him to be free, to play, to eat cactus leaves and fruits, and to make friends—it was a time for adventure and fun.

A curious gaze into the history of my family tree revealed to me unresolved traumatic events and feelings—abandonment, despair, isolation, aggression, and anxiety—unwittingly passed from one generation to the next. Understanding our intergenerational trauma is crucial to making sense of the origins of our behaviors and attitudes.

When my parents met and married, it was with the shared goal of being happy and building a long-lasting family—an experience that had been denied them as children. However, when my parents started living together, they didn't only bring a suitcase full of hopes and harmonious expectations; they brought with them another suitcase packed with unspoken fears and broken hearts. Both my parents had survived the loss of their parents and endured emotional deprivation as part of their lives as orphans at NPH. While they received caring attention from many amazing people in the orphanage, that attention was not comparable to the attention a child could have received from caring parents.

As a child, I witnessed and suffered the unskillful ways in which they expressed their frustrations and the scars they carried with them as a result of their own family history. As children, it's difficult to understand and to question where our parents' yelling, depression, and aggression come from. We only feel the effects of their unresolved pain. In the same way our parents transfer their genetic information on to us, they transfer—albeit unintentionally—the traumas that shaped their personal stories and attributes as individuals.

I never really questioned why my mother had a bad temper most of the time or why my father was emotionally inexpressive. The yelling, the punishments, the tears running down my mother's face, and my father's absences all became part of the normal landscape of our childhood. It wasn't until later I started to connect the dots and make sense of the emotional heritage of my intergenerational family.

For my mom, the retelling of her stories helped her to heal in some way; maybe every time she shared her story, she could see her resilience and ability to get to where she is today. In the stories my mom shared with me, her continuous effort to excel and to achieve, in spite of her pain and fatigue, was evident. The other crucial ingredient that helped her overcome obstacles was her spirituality. My mom, her mother, and grandmother were devoted Catholic women who had a strong belief in God's ability to protect and positively intervene and guide their lives. My faith was also built through the stories and actions of these women in my intergenerational family. During part of my childhood years, my great grandmother Consuelo babysat me and my brothers. During that time, she nurtured my faith in God and made sure we fulfilled at least some of the basic sacraments.

The female characters in my mother's stories were faithful, serving women whose hearts were capable of unconditional love. My curious gazing into my mother's narratives helped me understand the events that shaped her life and the ways in which she was able to relate to my brothers and me emotionally. In revising the echoes of my past, I didn't only realize the intergenerational trauma; I also uncovered the stories of unconditional love and strength of which the women of my family were the heroes.

Understanding and welcoming my past wouldn't be complete without curiously gazing the intergenerational heritage I received from my father. Although my father doesn't have as many stories to tell as my mother, the stories he has shared with me have been very meaningful toward understanding him and the ways he makes sense of life. My father liked to tell us stories about running in the fields, eating raw vegetables, playing with insects, and being free as a child. Unlike my mom who was born and raised in Mexico City, my father was born in a rural town in the state of Morelos, located in the central part of Mexico and known for its amazing natural landscapes. From his stories, I was mesmerized by my father's accounts about his father's psychic abilities. I have always been captivated by that mystical world and the ways in which life is explained.

According to my father, my grandfather knew how to do *limpias* (spiritual cleansings), read tarot cards, and work with spiritual mediums. While my father doesn't recall a lot about his parents, he enjoyed telling us about the ways in which his father made sense of life through his particular point of view as a healer. As a result, I developed an inclination and natural curiosity to understand the mysticism of life and of the possibility to interpret life beyond the logic of rational science.

With my mom being born in one of the largest cities in Mexico and my father being born in a rural area in Morelos, my childhood was defined by an appreciation of the rationality of cities as well as the spirituality that transpires in rural towns. Both landscapes became equally valuable to me. Diving deep into the stories my parents have shared with me throughout my life has been an amazing gift because it allowed me to understand my roots and to make sense of where some of the attributes of my identity come from.

My parents' storytelling doesn't end with stories of their childhood. They also shared with me many stories about their teenage years, their friends in the orphanage, past lovers, about how they met, and when and how they decided to get married. Although my mom has been the one to initiate family storytelling, my father also enjoys being asked about his life. Being the curious person I am, I rarely miss a chance to ask my parents to share their stories.

Curiously gazing our family stories can help us find not only the roots of our struggles but also the love that created us and the possibilities for our growth. The stories of our predecessors carry a strong power that lies dormant until we tap into it. When we learn the stories that made us, we have more resources to understand who we are and so decide who we can become.

When I started to make sense of my mother's family stories, I was able to understand the roots of her chronic depression, her disciplinary style, and her difficulty to express affection. Knowing her stories helped me understand and forgive her mistakes and see her as a human being who, despite her traumatic past, was able to live life and do the best she could to create a family.

In my mother's stories, it became evident that love meant a creative energy capable of resisting adversity. Her way of loving someone is to endure, persist, and to be successful so as to provide a good life for them. My mom was not an affectionate person who would say, "I love you." However, her love for me and my two brothers was embedded in the perpetual resilience with which she met and conquered every day. It was her love for us that helped her overcome depression on a daily basis—sometimes more successfully than at other times—to keep us going. My mother's stories are about stubborn, resilient problem solving. I learned from her that giving up is not an option; there is always a way.

Learning about my father's stories helped me understand why he struggled to be both expressive and communicative. Losing his parents when he was a very young boy meant he didn't have enough time with them to learn how to receive or express affection. My father learned to use self-isolation and journeys into nature as ways to escape the pain and confusion he felt at the loss of his parents and his transfer to the orphanage.

Even as a parent, my father maintained his distance. However, when I looked closer into his stories, I found a man who was sensible and noble, someone who wasn't ambitious or aggressive, a man who allowed himself to appreciate nature and enjoy life's simple pleasures. I found someone who was equable and patient—both essential skills when observing spiders and lizards in the backyard.

His stories and my daily observations of my father while I was growing up revealed a quiet man who enjoyed reading by himself at home and who honored knowledge as much as nature. He was an observant man who relished silence and could entertain himself easily. He knows more than he is willing to share sometimes, and—when given the chance—he can explain the intricate nature of things in life. I learned from him that silence and observation are essential tools with which to conquer life.

The curious gazing of our intergenerational families and the stories of our parents are crucial to understand not only the wounds we may have inherited but also the creative force that brings us here today. From my father, I learned the curiosity to observe. From my mom, I learned the persistent gaze that looks for understanding. As parents share their stories with their children, they are offering a tool for self-understanding, intergenerational understanding, and family pride.

Family storytelling also enables children to nurture a more compassionate view of their parents. When we understand the struggles our parents have endured, we can learn to forgive and to admire them as human beings.

The power of family storytelling and curious gazing combined resides in the possibility to identify the building blocks that sustain our being, and the miraculous mix of events that conspired to create who we are today. We need to learn and honor the stories that have created us; we need to be grateful for the good and the bad that comes with our family heritage. We must appreciate at each point of the chronology of our creation there is the expression of creative energy: the love that brought us here today.

4

GAZING OUR FAMILY DYNAMICS: THE ROLES WE PLAY AND THE LOVE WE SHARE

In the previous chapters, I have explained the importance of acknowledging oneself as an area for curious gazing. The possibility for self-understanding and self-growth is initiated when we turn inward to examine who we are and consider who we can become. However, curious gazing goes beyond self-awareness and self-examination; it also includes the critical examination of the society in which we live.

Although there are many social and cultural dimensions to life, one valuable branch of exploration is the area of gender expectations to which individuals in society have to respond. I emphasize, both men and women living in today's modern society struggle to satisfy competing demands—a struggle that can ultimately lead to psychological distress.

We went on to look at how curious gazing involves diving into our past and the stories of our intergenerational families to better understand the roots of our being and, most importantly, the creative energy that brought us to where we are today.

Finally, in addition to tracing the origins of our strengths and dispositions, curious gazing should help us make better sense of the role we play in our family dynamics and the meaning we attach to it. Gazing our family dynamics is crucial to understand the attributes of our personality at the present moment, our styles of attachment, and the skills we have as well as those we lack. Our family is our first arena for socialization; we learned a lot about how to behave socially and emotionally through the roles we enacted in our family from childhood to the present.

By looking a little deeper into my own family dynamics and my realizations, we will see how it's possible to look back and make sense of the ways in which our family dynamics shape us.

In gazing my family dynamics, I realized from a relatively young age I had to become another adult in the house to help my parents sustain our family life. Both my parents had to work as schoolteachers and their work time, job places, and workload made it difficult to be present all the time. This meant me assuming multiple responsibilities I was neither prepared for nor aware of their relevance in the functioning of my family.

As time passed by, leaving home—along with my graduate education and therapy—gave me intellectual and emotional tools to step back and examine my relationship with my family. With renewed understanding, I slowly realized that during most of my teenage years and beyond I had experienced a process of *parentification*, a term coined describing the alteration of family dynamics whereby a child plays the role of caregiver—of siblings or of the parents themselves.[6]

Parentification occurs when the family unit (parents and children) experience adverse conditions that force them to alter the natural or logical hierarchy of the family so as to preserve some sense of stability. Parentification can have long term effects on the physical and mental health of children who experience it, including a greater risk of anxiety, depression, chronic physical illness, difficulties in establishing relationships, and an inappropriate sense of entitlement.

When I was in the fifth grade of elementary school, my parents decided we needed to move from one state to another. They didn't like the level of pollution and social environment of the place where we used to live so as to guarantee a cleaner and healthier environment for their children, we moved to the city of Cuernavaca in the state of Morelos, Mexico. In doing so, my mother had to quit her tenure teaching job (she didn't have the option to relocate) and move with my brothers and me to a house that was still in the process of being built. My father had to stay in Mexico City to keep working and sustain the family.

For the next eight years, my parents lived apart, only meeting over weekends. This caused them to struggle, not only with their parenting practices but also in their relationship. Her role as the only caregiver of three children was very hard for my mom, and she was also depressed about not being employed for the first time in her adult life. For the first couple of years, she searched persistently for a new job. As a family, we endured financial hardship as well as a sense of instability and insecurity.

With my father's weekly absences, I had no choice but to become the helping hand my mom required and the substitute father my brothers needed. My teenage years and my early 20s were not times of fun and romantic exploration as one would normally expect. Instead, I had to learn to be committed, trustworthy, reliable, disciplined, creative, and empathetic.

My parents did their best to be with us as much as possible, given the resources they had available at the time. However, life's demands needed to be fulfilled and the alteration of our family roles would take its toll on every one of us. Although I was older than my brothers, I hardly knew how to guide and sustain them during the time they were under my charge at home.

While the impact of parentification in my life and that of my family is real, it's crucial to note that plunging into premature adulthood also equipped me with important skills and dispositions toward life. I think hardship has an element of life preparation that can hardly be replicated in the best pedagogically infused classroom. The level of problem-solving that was required of me forced me to develop an agile mind, the ability to multitask, the disposition to read people's behavior and emotions, patience to organize and coordinate people, time management, and creativity to maneuver everyday life without hurting anybody in the process.

I learned to collaborate with my mom on everything it took to keep the house in order. She taught me about budgeting for a household, to save for emergencies, to prioritize expenses, and to make smart purchases. I learned to cook and to babysit my brothers. Helping my brothers do their homework every day, I learned to become a teacher long before I went to college. As my father only came home for the weekends, he had the joy of being the parent who could do fun activities with us, while my mom carried the heavy responsibility of daily parenting discipline.

While my parents struggled to find the best parenting practices to raise us, they also did many good things. Even when my mom was overwhelmed—which was often—she always found time to promote the value of education and support our school commitments. She paid great attention to stimulating our creativity and learning skills, to eat healthily, to be disciplined and reliable, and to be morally sound. She also taught us to engage in artistic and small entrepreneurial activities.

My father made sure my brothers and I had something to read, bringing us new or different books and tales. He also encouraged us to be active and to engage in sports. He was supportive of our fantasies and desires. He made us feel that having fun was an important part of life. He read us bedtime stories and took us on walks with our dogs.

I know my mom carries a heavy burden within herself for the multiple times her depression and frustration got the better of her and she lashed out at us. I hope one day she will truly forgive herself and understand that I saw and valued her tireless efforts and love for us, even if she didn't always find the best ways to communicate it.

Parenting is an extremely challenging experience and I honor my parents' courage to bring three new lives into this world and to give us the chance to do something great with our lives. They have nothing to feel guilty about. They did the best they could; now it is our time to mend ourselves.

In the story of my family, the role of my brothers in my life is irreplaceable. While we live two countries apart now, my brothers remain a part of my everyday life. Our bond became strong because my parents taught us to protect and support each other. We have struggled together and worked together through the instability and distress that shaped our family life.

Leaving my brothers to pursue my professional aspirations in another country felt like tearing my heart in half. After all, I had lived with and loved them as both brothers *and* my own children. When I gaze our story, I realize it is one of true brotherhood. Our relationship is far from perfect; we fight and get mad at each other sometimes. The uniqueness of our relationship is not the absence of conflict but the ability to forgive and to love beyond our imperfections. It is based on the willingness to inspire each other to grow and take care of each other, even from a distance.

Growing up, my brothers had to deal with their own share of pain and struggles. Like me, the emotional deprivation and sense of abandonment they experienced affected them. As the older sister, I try to help them realize the greatness that lies within them and the importance of moving beyond negative emotions and self-destructive behaviors to grow as individuals.

While I have had lots to share with them and teach them, I've also learned from and grown through them. As time passes,

I continue to learn to be more their sister than their mother figure. I keep learning to respect and appreciate their individuality and capacity to choose and create their own destinies. Rodolfo is the middle child; he's four years younger than me. Rodolfo is strong and courageous, even if that hurts him sometimes. He loves sports and he is the most talented of us all in that field. His ability and interest in sports led him to become a physical instructor, a role he's held for more than a decade. He has incredible skills to bond with children and motivate them to endure.

Rodolfo is the most affectionate of the three of us. He enjoys receiving affection and acknowledgment. He uses humor to convey his emotions; it's his safe way to express what he feels.

Rodolfo, like my mother, is a tireless warrior. He is keen to realize the opportunities for growth that he has ahead of him. When I've had difficult times, he has reminded me I am valuable and unique. Rodolfo teaches me the importance of endurance and of believing in ourselves beyond our mistakes. He encourages me to dare to live life to the fullest.

Rodolfo dares to live, love, and express himself to the fullest. I see in him a man who is capable of redefining traditional ways of being a man (strong, fearless, unattainable) to become a loving partner to his wife Deborah, an introspective individual, and a tender and caring father to his baby son Enzo. He is a source of inspiration, faith, and support for me. As time keeps moving, I observe with pride his journey into a process of growth as an individual and now a creator of life along with his partner.

Oscar is the youngest of the three of us; he's six years younger than me. He is brave in his own unique way. His style of daring life is not loud but silent. He has always been more in touch with his feminine side, which became a cause for bullying at some point during his early school years. He cares for all forms of life and appreciates opportunities to serve others. As an undergraduate student, he chose art as his major. He has a creative and sensitive soul. When committed to his craft, he exhibits amazing talent.

Acknowledging, embracing, and negotiating his homosexuality has been both a challenging and enriching journey for Oscar. Being prone to serious introspection and philosophical thought, he sometimes gets overwhelmed with his thoughts and imagination. However, he always comes back with new insights and with a reconfigured sense of who he is. Oscar is a very smart man with a sharp memory and a talent for learning different languages. While he finds joy in solitude, his soul craves for companionship and opportunities to socialize.

Oscar is brave to explore the world even though sometimes the infinite possibilities of the future make him a bit anxious. He is a silent but persistent observer of the world. He surprises me with the knowledge he possesses. He reminds me about the importance of pausing and paying attention to life. He makes me feel listened to when I am afraid or in pain. He is a resilient man whose experiences of exclusion and depression have shown me the strength of the human spirit. He shares with me a passion for the mystical world, the inexplicable coincidences of life, and the messages of dreams.

In addition to my brothers, I have a sister by choice. My cousin Raquel is the daughter of my father's brother, who is an additional father figure to me. Uncle Roberto lived with my parents when I was born and helped raise me for the first five or six years of my life. When my parents were busy, he was there for me. A disciplined person with solid core values such as honesty, solidarity, service, commitment, and loyalty, he has remained a caring and supporting figure in my life. When I was a child, he often took me with him on walks around the neighborhood. He valued exercise and instilled that as an important habit. He has always been an amazing male role model for me and my brothers. He has always been a pillar in my life.

Although Raquel is ten years younger than me, she is a very mature and smart lady. One of my best friends, she is my cheerleader, confidant, and advisor. Every time we have a good conversation, she teaches me something about life. I can talk to her about everything that concerns me. We share a passion for dogs and an interest in the esoteric and natural worlds. We care for each other and do our best to make sure we communicate the love we share. By listening to me, she makes me feel valued.

In gazing my relationships with my family members, I learned to pay attention to the ways in which we have built our interactions and stories together. Observing the lives we co-create with our family members gives us an opportunity to learn more about ourselves, the roles we decide to play, and the energy we put into the world. As we engage in our family dynamics, we bring both our best and our worst. Few people in life will be able to know us to the depth that our parents and siblings know us.

Each family is a laboratory in which we learn how to give and receive love; there, we develop the foundations of our attachment style for future relationships. By accepting, rejecting, forgiving, forgetting, and remembering our parents and siblings, we cultivate ways to be with ourselves and with others. Our family unit is our first step into a social life; therefore, our ability to examine its past and build its present is crucial. The pillars of our mental health and our capacity to love others is rooted in the family environment to which we belong. It's essential to gaze this microcosm curiously, with the aim of noticing not only the mistakes and shortfalls but also the immense love and resiliency our family unit expresses as a group. Greater opportunities for self-awareness and self-growth rely on our ability to compassionately and intelligently observe the unique configurations of the nest that welcomed us into this world.

As I reflect on the family dynamics in which I have been immersed during my life, I can see both the good and the bad. Understanding the psychological components of my family history and configuration helped me understand and forgive my parents' unintentional mistakes. Most importantly, it helped me honor my parents' lives that are characterized by love, resiliency, and compassion.

My family prepared me to navigate the complexities of a contemporary world. My parents and my brothers have been the biggest life masters I have encountered in this place. Understanding my family dynamics enabled me to see others with compassion and a desire to learn about their roots and the depth of their wounds. Through the relationship I have with my family, I have learned to love beyond judgment, resentment, or pain. Only families can teach these types of things; there is no equivalent school curriculum that can touch the deepest fibers of our soul.

Our families are one of the richest sources of learning and self-construction. Parents and children have not only the responsibility but also the privilege to examine each other's stories—not from a judgmental position but rather a compassionate place that can promote their mutual understanding and growth.

PART I: SUMMARY

Curious gazing is the disposition by which we can look inwards, backwards, and onwards in our lives with the intention to learn, grow, and build more conscious and compassionate connections with ourselves and other people.

When we develop a life disposition embracing critical awareness, curiosity, and compassion, it becomes possible to uncover important layers of meaning in our personal stories. Curious gazing can guide us to realize the greatness that exists within us, our world, our intergenerational families, and our family dynamics. As a life disposition, curious gazing is something we can practice and refine every day. The more we engage in it, the better we can become at it.

We can practice gazing our society by paying attention to cultural traditions and values. Our analysis of gender dynamics, racial tensions, social class differences and inequalities in the world we live in can help us understand our social position in society and the ways in which we want to participate in it.

We can curiously gaze our intergenerational families by engaging our parents and grandparents in conversations. We can ask them about their stories, their past, find out about turning points in their lives, and ask them what they've learned from their past or what wounds their past has left them. A good practice is to draw our family tree, identifying both the traumatic and glorious events in our story line. We can then pay attention to the people in our families who have been excluded as a result of those traumas, or embraced as a result of love.

Gazing our family dynamics enables us to understand the roles we play and the relationships we've built. By analyzing specific events, practices, and relationships from our family history, we can understand the source of some of our behaviors, ways of thinking, and emotions.

Curious gazing, which includes a compassionate and critical reflection of ourselves, our present and past, is foundational to discover the creative force (love) that was used to create and sustain our personal stories. Beyond the pain, the struggles, the mistakes, and the cultural mandates, life finds a way to manifest and to perpetuate generation after generation. I am certain part of our purpose in this life is to make a pause in our busy daily routines and examine our lives. We will find immense value in learning the stories of our origins, the stories that shape us today, and the stories of love that sustain us in the midst of challenging times.

PART 2

REALIZING OUR CREATIVE ENERGY: THE LOVE THAT LIVES WITHIN US

NOTES FROM A HUMMINGBIRD

*We are creative energy that enables the authoring of a
life, a lasting love, and a resilient world. In our ability to
acknowledge and own our power resides the seed of infinite
transformation.*

In this part of the book, I will talk to you about my story of
self-development. I will share some of the most significant
stories of my life that helped me become who I am today.
In sharing my story of self-growth and the process of my
self-actualization, I want to show how each one of us is capable of achieving higher levels of awareness, confidence, and
accomplishment. Through my account, I want to emphasize
authentic growth is not always easy or enjoyable; it demands
courage and it takes time and effort.

I am not attempting to represent myself as a model of
self-perfection. On the contrary, my personal and intimate
stories will show the vulnerability and imperfection that defines
any process of self-construction. Becoming stronger and more
confident is the outcome of continual self-making; it is never
finished; it is never perfect.

Through my stories, I will show both the fragility and the
resiliency that exist within each of us. I will talk about my
personal struggles, internal turmoil, and fears that challenged

me as I tried to make sense of who I am and the things I want out of life. In addition, I will also share stories of success, personal conquests, confidence, and gratitude that helped me build internal strength. You will learn about the key experiences, relationships, and realizations that made it possible for me to reach higher levels of self-understanding (awareness), autonomous decision-making (internal voice and authority), and compassionate interaction with others (collaboration and service).

As I talk about my personal journey, I will describe specific approaches that may help you in your own process of self-growth. Two components of this next part of the book will be particularly useful in helping you identify self-improvement strategies. The first component is a description of the three pathways to reconnect with the inner self: unconditional self-acceptance, self-compassion, and self-admiration. The second component discusses eight types of creative projects to enrich and empower yourself.

The creative projects refer to a concrete series of practices in which each one of us can engage to improve who we are by learning something new and creating something out of it. These creative projects are a product of two things: an active state of mind seeking growth, and a compassionate examination of the lesson learned within each of the stories we have lived. When I looked back at my stories, I realized it was important to find the hidden lessons and understand how these could lead to new practices or habits to author stories of self-empowerment.

As you read my personal story, I invite you to consider the ways in which it inspires you to think about and examine your own personal story, and contemplate your own experiences of struggle and resilience. As you dive into your personal journey, I encourage you to explore the ways in which the examination of your stories can help you reach higher levels of self-understanding (awareness), autonomous decision-making (internal voice and authority), and compassionate social interaction (collaboration and service).

While the stories I will share are about a female character, I am certain many of my experiences will resonate with men too. Self-development is not an exclusively female practice; males can also benefit and engage in the process.

Engaging in a conscious effort to examine who we are and to pursue personal growth is a crucial endeavor in current times. We tend to disregard ourselves as objects of contemplation, examination, and authoring because we are so busy doing a million other things. However, there is much beauty and creative energy within us that deserve to be acknowledged. Practices like mindfulness and meditation are constantly calling us to stop and position ourselves in a place of appreciation and gratitude. It is from that place of appreciation and gratitude we can use curious gazing to realize the creative energy living within us. It is the activation or use of our creative energy—the love within—that allows us to author ourselves consciously and purposefully.

5

CAUGHT BETWEEN SACRIFICE AND DESIRE: LEARNING TO ERASE ONESELF

A crucial element in the story of my life is the strong presence of my mother. Both science and spirituality acknowledge mothers play a big part in shaping who we are.[7] My mother has been amazing in many ways: she is a great ambassador of unconditional love and service to others, a stoic family pillar, skillful chef, clever professional, inspiring muse, and forgiving creature. She is the best lie detector, creative artist, and cancer survivor. Of course, she has some imperfections like any other human being.

My mom often said her job as a mother was to create productive and moral citizens for society. As a result, she put discipline and respect for authority at the top of her list of values to instill. She set high standards for my brothers and me and encouraged us to reach them. Truth be told, sometimes her style of encouragement wasn't always the best. I characterize my mother's parenting style as mostly strict, based on firm rules, low tolerance of mistakes, emphasis on instilling obedience, and high demands. While she had moments of caring and affectionate communication, she was a demanding mother.

Thinking back carefully, I believe the years my mom was forced to live alone with us exacerbated her style. She probably felt, given the absence of my father, she had to play the stern role. With my mom being one of the strongest forms of attachment I built as a child, it became natural for me to be disciplined, obedient, and silent.

In addition to my mom's parenting style, our family environment was far from stable or stress-free. As a child, teenager, and then young adult, I experienced constant anxiety, which was associated to the conditions under which my parents constructed their relationship as a couple and as parents. They married young (in their early 20s) and their firstborn—me—came the first year after they got married. Although both of them had an educational career and a job, they were beginners in the business of family life. With limited time to adjust to marriage and parenting, and dragging years of emotional deprivation, they started their family with limited support and knowledge with which to negotiate their life as a couple, their commitment as parents, and financial constraints. As a result, my brothers and I ended up with a mother who felt overworked and unloved, and a father who probably felt clueless about how to engage in caring fatherhood and become a loving husband.

While my mother struggled in her role as housekeeper and primary caregiver, my father spent his working weeks away alone, with no parenting responsibilities until weekends. As time passed, this dynamic took its toll on everyone. For my parents, it created a psychosocial entanglement of frustration, depression, loneliness, and dissatisfaction.

In this unbalanced context, I became a premature adult and an anxious girl who constantly worried about emerging conflicts. To calm the anxiety, I have constantly tried to be the moderator, the voice of reason, and the calm person when everyone else is yelling at each other. To compensate the constant conflict I experienced in my family environment,

I became quiet and avoided expressing anger and conflict. I learned to mute my emotions because in the midst of family conflict there wasn't time to listen to my needs and concerns as a child, teenager, and later as an adult. This doesn't mean I never had a chance to talk about my needs or desires with my parents; I did. But unfortunately, that wasn't the norm.

Being an anxious child and premature adult would cause me to struggle to interact with people of my own age. I wasn't a social pariah at school; I had friends but I did experience bullying because I was too responsible and too "well behaved." At every stage of my life, I have often engaged with my peers as though I was some sort of designated driver—the one who can't entirely relax because they have to make sure everyone else is behaving responsibly. I was hyper vigilant of risk-taking behaviors and did my best to avoid all types of irresponsible actions.

Under pressure to maintain high standards, I learned to rely on self-control and delayed gratification as a rule in my life. I became very self-disciplined, mostly because I didn't want to create more work for my mom with the potential consequences of any sort of irresponsible behavior.

With a clear mission and unquestioning desire to make my family proud, I worked every day to be the perfect daughter, sister, and student. In my attempts to help my mother and so to alleviate her burdens, I put myself under a lot of pressure. With my quest for perfection, a big, internalized self-critic emerged as an eternal companion in my life. Alongside my internal self-critic, I adopted the role of savior of my family. I shouldered the responsibility for everyone in my family being okay.

One of my primary motivations for leaving my family to study abroad was to help my family. I wanted to go back to Mexico and help them financially. I didn't want them to struggle for money. My reasoning was if they had money, they would fight less, they would take therapy, and they would be more at peace. I wanted them to be happy, to live peacefully, and to enjoy vacations for the first time in their lives. My mind was set on one goal: achieving for my family.

With that clarity of mind, I forgot I existed. I unconsciously erased the possibility of achieving for myself. My motivation to help my family kept me going through the next five years of loneliness, struggles, and heavy workloads. I felt fortunate to have received a scholarship from my country and I was determined not to lose it.

From 2005 to 2010, I became a professional woman whose desire to serve others (my family) made her excel in everything she did. Paradoxically, the more professional I grew, the more I forgot about myself as a person. My desire to help my family was so consuming I forgot to enjoy the process. Through my mother, I had learned the cultural female prototype of sacrifice—putting others before yourself—was the way to be. Consequently, I viewed my period of studying abroad as a sacrifice I had to make for my family. For quite some time, having fun was out of the equation for me. I felt I couldn't get distracted and risk failure as that would mean failing my family too. I couldn't be selfish.

Building my new, professional self while studying abroad, I became both buried and alive. I buried many of my desires and needs, choosing instead to blindly pursue this experience that would primarily benefit others. Simultaneously, I became alive because the intellectual work I was doing opened the doors to new concepts and knowledge that would later help me to re-discover myself.

As I reflect on some of the stories I've shared with you, I can attest to the slow, steady process of erasing oneself to prioritize the existence of others. Be assured I'm not saying it's wrong to build a sense of service to and solidarity with our families. On the contrary, I am in support of strengthening family ties and solidarity. There is a fine line, however, between service and self-erasure. And it's risky not to carefully maintain the delicate balance between giving and receiving, self-preservation and service.

When I adopted the role of "family savior" I wasn't consciously aware of what that meant or of the outcome for me. Nobody asked me to make that sacrifice. However, my psychological state took me to assume that role voluntarily, mainly because I felt it was my responsibility after witnessing my parents' everyday efforts and sacrifices. My parents have never asked me to sacrifice my life for theirs. However, when we are younger, nobody explains how to navigate the struggles we live. We do our best given the personal resources available to us at the time.

At the same time my self-erasure was orchestrated, my process of self-realization and self-growth started to bloom slowly and steadily. Opportunities of self-awakening brought me to a new encounter with myself. In the process of becoming new, there are multiple moments in which one can discover an improved version of the person we used to be. While self-erasure took a toll on my being, the process of re-writing my identity has been a challenging yet rewarding experience.

6

THE CONJURING OF THE ALPHA WOMAN: THE CHARADE OF UNTAMED FEARS

My decision to be the first woman in my family to pursue a doctoral degree and to leave my family to live in a foreign country involved multiple challenges. One of those challenges was having to question traditional gender stereotypes, cultural traditions, and even nationalistic values. Once in a foreign country, I quickly realized I had to redefine myself to fit in, which wasn't easy at all.

I arrived in California when I was 23 years old. I had never been to the United States before. In fact, I'd hardly visited any other state in my own country. Only once or twice in my life I'd had the opportunity to visit one of the most popular beaches in Mexico—Acapulco. My family never really had the opportunity to go on vacation to any place. Therefore, the cultural shock of moving to the United States was intense.

I was probably the youngest graduate student in my cohort. There were only two international students in the group: a Taiwanese lady and me. From the first day, I felt the pressure to look smart, be productive, and dress properly. Every day was another chance to conquer the new world and to improve myself in some way.

During this initial stage, the presence of my dear friend Anna—another Latina woman in the program—became one of my biggest supporters. She made me feel included and supported through the process, opening her heart and her family to help me feel welcomed. Her help was extremely valuable and unforgettable. Anna was always kind but she also knew when to challenge me to grow.

One of my first tests as a foreign graduate student was to sound smart. Like any other person learning a second language later in life, I had (and still do have) a marked accent. Learning to speak and write academic English was my main mission. It took me the first year of my stay as a graduate student to effectively communicate my ideas. In every class conversation, every assignment, and every meeting with a professor, I felt like I was going to war and my self-esteem was one of the biggest casualties. Even when I felt I'd conquered English grammar, I didn't feel confident when speaking or writing English.

Social scenarios were even worse. I knew the rules of being a good student, but being *outside* that academic framework with girls and guys was a whole different story—I didn't have a clue how to behave. My survival strategy was twofold: I put as much work as possible into become an academically proficient student, and I chose to retreat myself from social scenarios to avoid feelings of discomfort and shame. While an elegant and pragmatic prescription, all work and no play would prove not to be the best pathway for a healthy life.

In my efforts to improve my academic skills and language proficiency, I started to work as a research assistant, a job I undertook to help practice and improve my writing skills in a second language. With this new job, my workload grew exponentially. The part-time job gave me the opportunity to work with a professor, John, who would become my mentor. He took me under his wing to guide me in the ways of the capricious and intricate academic world. He taught me about professional ethics, discipline, and productivity. He held high standards and I was committed to reach each benchmark he set for me.

John and his wife, Lee, became pillars of my formation as a professional. They not only supported my academic growth and guided me to consolidate my academic work, they also welcomed me into their lives and showed me an unexpected level of respect and compassion. I will always have an immense sense of appreciation and gratitude for them. They made me feel I had a family away from home.

John is a committed scholar, a disciplined instructor, and a serious thinker. Great explorers, John and Lee are intellectual people and avid travelers who have a wealth of stories they keenly share about their trips around the world. They showed an amazing humility and readiness to learn about my country, my personal story, and my family. Both of them are eager to learn about other cultures and regions. They value all forms of art and are willing to share their knowledge and faith in humanity with others. Being part of their lives has been a privilege.

During my years as a graduate student, I overworked. Work became the perfect escape from having a personal and social life. Other than doing exercise and having a couple of friends, most of my life was spent studying and working. Although over the years I received invitations to different social events, most often I almost automatically declined. I was always busy; there was no time for parties, no time for adventures, and definitely no time for guys.

For many years, weekday and weekends were the same world for me. Getting up at 6am and going to bed at 11pm was my daily routine, from Monday to Sunday, for six long years. I felt I couldn't waste any time; I had to work hard. I had a clear goal in mind: helping my family. To overcome my impostor syndrome, I worked harder than everybody else.

By the end of my doctoral degree, this rigid work ethic brought me important benefits. I had co-authored a book with my mentor one year before finishing a 350-page dissertation. I had presented research papers at several conferences and co-authored some book chapters. I had certainly been productive. In my constant race for efficiency and productivity, I had become an overachiever to silence my fear of failure.

Having conquered the fields of efficiency and productivity, there was still another challenge I had to face: to look pretty. Living in Southern California made me aware of different-forms of hair styling and makeup I'd never witnessed before. California girls, I observed, were committed to looking pretty. Physical beauty was a sensitive topic for me because I'd never perceived myself as a beautiful girl. In my extended family, I was constantly compared to one of my cousins whose beauty was celebrated by everyone. We were almost the same age but, compared to her, I was given the label "*la chistosita*" (the cute, funny one).

It did not help that, on more than one occasion, my mom had lamented, "*Hubieras sacado mis dientes y mis cejas.* If only your teeth and eyebrows looked more like mine." I had misaligned teeth and gaps that caused me to avoid laughing in public. I also had freckles that evoked bullying at school and among my male cousins. To top it all off, in my early 20s I had to start wearing glasses. All of these things combined caused me to feel extremely insecure about my physical appearance. I was often mad at my parents for not making me prettier.

For many years, I never felt worthy of male attention because of my physical appearance. If by now you are picturing me as a Picasso painting, I would ask you to refrain. Science happened to me and after LASIK eye surgery, braces, makeup, and maybe good karma, I managed to arrive at a place of greater physical comfort.

Going relentlessly to the gym was also part of my beautification project. Like many other women pressured by the mainstream values of beauty, I was anxious about the possibility of gaining weight; therefore, in addition to a regular exercise routine, I learned about nutrition to manage a healthy body weight. By my late 20s, I wasn't completely confident about my image yet, but I was able to look in the mirror with more acceptance. Looking back, the constant policing of my body and dedication to beautification was to silence the fear of rejection.

When I finished my doctoral degree and found a job as a professor, first in Mexico and then in the United States, I worked arduously every day to become the type of alpha female who embraced her leadership ambitions and was talented, confident, self-sufficient, and highly productive. In our contemporary world, there are multiple cultural and social mandates for women. We are each required to be superwoman—to be professionally driven, family oriented, independent and yet emotionally committed, confident and yet dependent on males too, ambitious but also service-oriented. My everyday life was my own version of fulfilling as many social and cultural expectations as I could, even if some of them were contradictory and almost impossible to satisfy.

In my business world, my trajectory of efficiency and productivity made it feasible for me to build a sense of confidence that became stronger and stronger as I overcame different professional challenges. I felt extremely proud of my work and career development. I felt I was efficient in my profession, an impression that was reaffirmed by my colleagues. In my job, I viewed myself as a leader and an expert who had valuable ideas to share with others. I enjoyed my line of work and I felt highly capable of helping students to learn.

My personal world was a different story. In the realm of my relationships with family and friends, I struggled to find the confidence to affirm myself and to believe in my value. From the outside, I probably looked the epitome of the alpha woman I was aiming to be: a woman confident enough to study abroad and live by herself, someone with leadership aspirations, and who was highly skilled and motivated. And yet, from the inside, my self-image and sense of self was crumbling.

The reality was I had so many fears I could classify them by color, size, or alphabetic order: fear of not being enough, fear of not being accepted and loved, fear of being alone, fear of being rejected because of my appearance, fear of losing the people I love, fear of failure, and even fear of dying. My fears had two allies to keep them afloat: the compulsion to overanalyze and the desire to control. Both these habits were not only easy to hide but were also rewarded in my profession.

A professor is required to be very careful about designing other people's learning opportunities and anticipating obstacles and solutions; therefore, having high analytical skills and the ability to control or regulate the effects of certain variables (motivation, cognitive demands, learning resources, etc.) was and continues to be very useful. In my personal life, however, overanalyzing and controlling made my pursuit of happiness more challenging—everyday life and relationships with people cannot always be subject to rationality and regulation.

Analyzing life and its various factors is not only useful but relevant to making sense of who we are. The disposition of curious gazing requires analytical skills. Nevertheless, over-analyzing can be detrimental to the mind and the spirit when one's thinking patterns encourage increased stress and anxiety.

Overanalyzing involves letting an uncontainable amount of beliefs, inferences, and imaginary ideas run wild without clear purpose or organization. This thought process can be associated to rumination or obsessive thinking, which involves obsessing about certain types of thoughts (mostly negative) regarding a present, past, or future life situation. Overanalyzing is risky when we get fixated in thinking reality must happen in exactly the same way we imagine it in our mind. The more we realize reality is far from functioning as we see it in our mind's eye, the more stress it creates in our lives.

At its worst, overanalyzing led me to mild panic attacks, fatalistic imaginings, and depression. My mind excels at making connections among multiple and even distant topics; sometimes I wish it could be less effective, particularly when the connections created lead me to very stressful scenarios. But effective it was and my compulsive thinking and negative visualizing led me to constantly police myself and others, and to create high expectations about things in life.

The most damaging effects of my overactive mind was my constant self-judgment. I was my own most unforgiving critic. Unintentionally, I also subjected others to my high expectations. I expected them to act in a certain way and was frustrated when that didn't occur.

In an uncertain world, a high degree of flexibility is a necessity and I was urged to address my thinking vices. If I wanted to heal myself and embrace a healthy approach to life, I would have to turn my mind into an ally and persuade my heart to jump into the bandwagon with us.

Therapy—as well as engaging in honest and hard conversations with my brothers and closest friends—was crucial toward realizing the charade of the alpha female and to embark on a search for a healthy integration of my professional and personal worlds. Up to that point, my heart had been ruled by my mind. I had learned to rely excessively on my rationality in my effort to gain a sense of control over my life. Now, I had to learn to listen to my heart and my emotions again without fear of getting lost in them.

When I reflect and examine the story of my life up to this point, I see myself as a woman who is still trying to embrace and accept herself fully. I have been able to conquer vast territory in the fields of self-acceptance and self-affirmation. I work every day with my mind and my heart to find the right balance with which to lead my life. Some days are easier to manage than others but I trust myself more and more each time. I am capable of contemplating myself and identifying when my mind is overacting or when my heart is being silenced. I haven't abandoned all my fears yet; however, I'm more willing to open the door to them and hear them talk. I can ask them what they need from me and how I may live a life of contentment if they are even latent in the back of my mind.

I have found every day is another chance to rediscover my value, to love myself more, to appreciate my creative energy, and to discover what I can offer to others from a place of contentment. Life is about finding balance again and again, after events and situations have stolen it from us. Through my personal journey, I realized my instability came from constant fear of multiple things, including myself. I also discovered stability comes from the ability to trust one's strength to overcome internalized, silent, and voracious fears.

7

THE VICES OF THE LONELY HEART: THE UNCOMFORTABLE CONQUEST OF SOLITUDE

One common characteristic of single professional women is their financial independence, which affords them the opportunity to live by themselves. Judging from the standards of the modern world, being capable of having a place to live independently is a sign of financial competency and maturity, both as an adult and a professional. Achieving this is one of the milestones of adulthood and brings with it a great sense of accomplishment. However, occupying a space where solitude and silence is part of everyday life can be a daunting experience.

I have lived as a self-sustained woman for almost two decades, solving life as it transpires. I lived with my family in Mexico until I was 23 years old, and then moved to California to undertake my graduate studies. As a doctoral student, I shared a living space with roommates; however, by the fifth year, I was finally able to afford living by myself. While having your own space can be very rewarding, the silence of an empty house or apartment can be uncomfortable and scary at times. Particularly when one uses solitude to engage in perpetual rumination or other similar vices.

In my personal experience, it was challenging adjusting to the loneliness because for most of my life I'd been used to being part of a collective (my family), and to functioning and operating with the benefit of the collective in mind. I was used to talk to someone for most of the day, to work as a team with my brothers, collaborate in shared projects, struggle together, and to support each other. All of a sudden, being alone meant I only had to worry about and focus on myself. Having no major responsibilities other than taking care of myself was a big privilege, but it also meant undergoing a huge process of re-interpreting my life, my priorities, and my concerns.

Despite the fact that for most of my time in the United States I've been physically alone, I've remained mentally and emotionally invested with my family in Mexico. We talk every day and whenever possible, they come to stay with me for several weeks at a time.

Inhabiting my solitude—first as a doctoral student and then as a single professional in a foreign country—wasn't easy. Happily, for the last nine years, I've had my little white poodle, Ted, to share the adventure. When I found myself living on my own and not having to operate as part of a collective, it took me some time before I was able to redirect my attention and energy toward viewing myself as a person worthy of attention and self-care. I struggled with unhealthy thinking habits that were exacerbated by being alone. My reflective musings were unrestrained, and fear, anxiety, lack of self-acceptance, and insecurity were rampant.

Rather than seeing and using solitude as a place for self-acknowledgement and celebration, I was cultivating my solitude as a fertile soil for toxic thinking. Being alone did not feel like a joyful experience. On the contrary, it was an energy-stealing experience and a space from which I needed to escape as quickly as possible. All the anxiety I felt about being alone started to manifest in physical symptoms such as muscle pain, back pain, panic attacks, colds, rashes, allergies, and gastric issues. The more I resisted my loneliness, the more difficult it felt to live in it.

Experiencing my solitude was uncomfortable, mainly because I had mixed feelings about it. On the one hand, I was very proud to be independent and to have a place of my own that showed the outcome of my hard work. On the other hand, my solitude became a space consumed with anxiety, self-doubt, and fear about different aspects of my life. Being alone meant spending long hours caught up in toxic thinking that created a foggy view about who I was.

When I reflect on the ways in which I inhabited my solitude, I realize I was lacking in self-awareness, self-compassion, and gratitude for life. In the silence of my solitude, I was being harsh on myself. I was not giving myself the opportunity to observe and value the fruits of my work, my value as a strong woman, and the creative energy within me that had enabled me to create the life opportunity I had at that moment.

In not acknowledging my creative work, I was being cruel and unfair to myself. I failed to admit the value and privilege of silence and personal space. A couple of times, some married friends pointed out to me I should be enjoying my solitude and my house because the life of a married man or woman can be very noisy. While I initially found their comment annoying or even unrealistic, life would show me there is a lot to appreciate in silence.

Reframing my attitude toward my solitude was essential toward healthier thinking habits and a wholesome life. This process of reframing didn't occur miraculously one day when I woke up. It took a series of deliberate acts to create a new narrative about myself. I had to be proactive in my desire to abandon toxic ways of thinking. I had to be aware of my desire to stop making life worse for myself. I realized I could choose what type of perspective I wanted to use to make sense of my life every day. I realized I could relearn how to inhabit my solitude. I could incorporate an asset perspective that would allow me to see my solitude as a place of opportunity to create, rather than as a place to bury myself.

Let's examine exactly how to do this.

8

RELEARNING TO INHABIT SOLITUDE: THREE PATHWAYS TO RECONNECT WITH THE INNER SELF

I learned from experience it is possible to walk the corridors of solitude in a healthier and more satisfying way. Relearning to inhabit my solitude took me along three pathways to reconnect with my inner self: unconditional self-acceptance, self-compassion, and self-admiration. Let me share with you what each of these pathways involves and why they are relevant. My description of each one of these pathways comes from my own process of self-discovery, nurtured by several creative projects in which I engaged.

To move into unconditional self-acceptance requires the silencing of outside voices, external opinions, social demands, and expectations. I want to clarify I am not making a case to ignore social rules or cultural traditions and values. There is value in our history as a socio-cultural community; however, silencing outside voices involves questioning the origins and nature of contemporary social mandates in popular media and society at large.

Unconditional self-acceptance requires us to listen to and trust an internal voice that says, "You are valuable and loved as you are." We live in a society where there is a constant demand for beauty, perfection, and productivity. In this context, it's not easy to accept who we are when our physical or personal traits don't match the mainstream ideals. It can be tempting to march under the sound of media pressure and external definitions of success. As an adult professional woman who was critical of social pressures and media, I still wanted to accomplish mainstream ideas of beauty and success and I experienced stress when my personal conditions didn't help me to reach those ideals.

Unconditional self-acceptance involves our ability to let go of external ideals or standards and instead create our own definitions of what beauty or success means, given our own personal stage and context. Based on a critical understanding of all the social messages around us, we can define what version of ourselves is important to pursue and build. Self-acceptance should promote constant self-improvement; however, it promotes it from an asset perspective. This means one has to look for self-improvement from a place where one already views oneself as valuable and lovable.

Self-acceptance begins with the understanding that human beings are equipped with amazing abilities and virtues that can be enriched even more. This position is different from a deficit perspective in which one wants to meet social expectations because there is a personal sense of lack. From a deficit perspective, one assumes one cannot be fully valuable until one reaches external formulas of success and beauty. Unconditional self-acceptance involves us being able to trust our personal resources and strengths to seek for an improved version of ourselves—a version that is healthy, balanced, and individually defined rather than socially imposed and demanded.

While self-acceptance implies an asset perspective in the search for self-improvement, self-compassion is a state of consciousness that views personal mistakes or setbacks as necessary ingredients in the process of self-improvement. As a woman who grew up under the demands of doing everything as perfectly as possible, I had a very difficult time allowing myself to make mistakes without feeling bad about them. Most of the time, I was very unforgiving of myself when things didn't turn out the way I expected. The result was a perpetual state of self-recrimination that caused constant stress and anxiety.

In my personal experience, embracing self-compassion has involved understanding I am not expected to be perfect, and mistakes or uncalculated effects are part of the process of growing. I had to learn to be more forgiving of myself, not judging my mistakes from a place of recrimination but rather appreciation.

Self-compassion doesn't mean a consent to be irresponsible or mediocre in our decision-making. Self-compassion relies on one's ability to engage in thoughtful decision-making, knowing our actions and decisions will be tempered by circumstances and that whatever comes, we can learn and reconfigure our next moves. In short, self-compassion is forgiving our mistakes from a place of appreciation that encourages learning rather than recrimination.

Self-admiration is the third component of the process of learning to inhabit oneself. Self-acceptance is embracing our birth-given virtues and ability to grow; self-compassion is the patience and appreciation to live with our actions and decisions. Self-admiration is a mindset based on the importance of acknowledging the value of our accomplishments and creative capacity.

Self-admiration is tied to the importance of celebrating our existence and our continual efforts to improve. This mindset does not advocate arrogance or entitlement. Instead, self-admiration is built from a place of humility and gratefulness. One needs humility to realize any type of self-improvement we reach is never an individual achievement but a collective accomplishment. We need to admire our ability to collaborate with others effectively in the construction of oneself and the world around us.

Self-admiration is also made up of our ability to appreciate our privileges: good health, able body, the roof over our heads, the job we have, the family group that loves us, and the place where we live. Self-admiration is tied to our ability to contemplate from a place of gratitude and realization of our creative capacity.

Self-acceptance, self-compassion, and self-admiration became crucial to learn how to inhabit my solitude in a healthier way. Embracing my solitude as something positive has been an intriguing, complex, and meaningful process leading to personal growth. Being willing to dive into one's personal dark places is not easy; however, it's very necessary to enable our move from a superficial understanding of who we are to a deeper realization of our inner selves.

I understand our inner self as a composite of creative energy (disposition toward creative work/action) and intuitive wisdom (disposition toward greater awareness) that is nurtured when we walk the three pathways I've discussed above. Solitude, as it turns out, can be a space to reconnect with our inner selves. The need to reconnect assumes that, somehow, we have been disconnected from it in the first place. In my view, the disconnection happens because of traumas (mild or wild) we experience.

From the moment we are born, we come in contact with people and circumstances that can either nurture or disconnect us from the love residing in and defining us. During our life journey, negative, unprocessed experiences can disconnect us from our inner selves. However, we also come into contact with experiences and people who encourage us to view and embrace ourselves from a place of higher self-acceptance, self-compassion, and self-admiration.

When we disconnect from our inner self, we start looking for acceptance, compassion, and admiration from the outside.

Reconnecting with our inner self involves looking inwards to gain self-awareness and self-appreciation. Solitude constitutes a persistent invitation to value and to re-configure our connection to our inner self.

9

EIGHT CREATIVE PROJECTS TO EMPOWER OUR INNER SELF

Walking the pathways of self-acceptance, self-compassion, and self-admiration were neither random events nor spontaneous occurrences. Rather, it took intentional desire to not live in depression, to learn more about myself, to confront my uncomfortable emotions of fear and anxiety, and to improve who I was. I had to learn to feel more comfortable with myself and to appreciate solitude as a space for self-construction.

Over the last two decades of my life, I have persistently explored eight creative projects as the means to reconnect with my inner self—specifically my creative energy and intuitive wisdom. Each one of these creative projects was built through continual learning and effort. In other words, behind each of these practices there was a clear desire to learn new mindsets and habits that would help me understand more about myself as a human being, as a woman, as a professional, as a spiritual being, and a member of society. Additionally, each of these projects was aimed to create and author a specific type of self. I was intentional in using these projects to actualize myself.

I use the notion of "creative project" to emphasize any effort to reconnect with our inner self and to grow personally

68

involves a course of action sustained by learning, continued effort, and a creative mission. A creative project is not a one-time action that has the capacity to solve a problematic situation at once. Instead, it is an articulated and intentional chain of actions enacted over time to create a richer, empowered self.

The eight creative projects I pursued are artistic expressions, therapy, scholarly and self-help books, spirituality, exercise, caring conversations, workshops, and podcasts. While the combination of these particular projects has been highly beneficial to me, each person will discover the right combination for them. Each person has to discover what type of creative projects work better for them. In what follows, I'll briefly share how I became engaged in each creative project and why they became relevant in the construction of who I am today. My description can help you understand how to approach each type of project and what you can gain from them.

ARTISTIC EXPRESSIONS

During my early 20s, I realized painting, art crafts, and writing were healing practices for me. Writing was a particularly salient way to help me process my emotions and thoughts. Especially when I was feeling sad, I found that writing poetry (in my own imperfect way) helped to purge negative emotions. I wrote for myself; it was an act of expressive liberation that helped me to put outside what was hurting inside. For a long time, I didn't feel comfortable sharing what I wrote until some of my friends read my poems and encouraged me to share them with others.

This book clearly shows my desire to keep using writing as a way to reach a higher understanding of my inner world. Since my poems were one of the ways that allowed me to process both negative and up-beat emotions, I have included one at the front of this book.

Writing about what we feel, think, or do in life has the power to reaffirm who we are in the world. The use of language as a tool for creative expression and personal recreation is powerful. When we use words to create something—a poem, a tale, an essay, a song—we are putting our voice into the outside world in an act of self-affirmation. Whether we are aware of it or not, through each word we put out there, we are saying to the universe, "Here I am; I am part of this world, I have something important to share, and I am capable of creatively authoring this journey with all of you."

Writing is an everyday practice for me. Both profession-ally and personally, I live through the things I write formally and informally. Words are not just *words*. They are my way of self-affirming my existence in this world. I use my words to build bridges, to teach something, to express who I am, and to communicate my amazement about this world.

My writing is a constant practice of personal making and re-making. Whether it is personal journaling, everyday text messaging, or authoring scholarly publications, words are a powerful tool to find myself and improve who I am as well as to show appreciation and connect with others. As an act of human expression, writing is a space for creativity. Through the use of words, each one of us can shape new universes, new pathways, and new encounters. Written language is one of the privileges we have as social creatures and as long as we can represent our ideas through the use of words, we have an infinite number of possibilities to expand who we are.

THERAPY

Similar to writing, seeing a therapist was a place for me to process the turmoil of my inner self. Different from the soli-tude of writing, therapy is a practice of companionship. For me, therapy was an opportunity to set time to listen to myself in a safe and guided environment. I decided to take therapy when I was able to afford it, which occurred during the time I was a graduate student abroad. My first experience with a therapist occurred in Mexico. When I was an international student in an American higher education institution, I didn't know about the free counseling services available to students. So, I was only able to attend therapy sessions every time I went back to Mexico during my vacation breaks at the end of each quarter.

My first therapist was a Mexican woman whose therapeutic approach emphasized the need for me to understand my past experiences, from my childhood. As a result, I was able to reflect on traumatic experiences from my childhood, my relationships with my parents, my relationship to authority figures, and my forms of romantic attachment. These sessions came to an end when I realized exploring my past and making sense of it wasn't enough for me anymore. I wanted to acquire concrete tools to help me modify my present, everyday life.

After a couple of years, I found another female therapist. Her approach attracted my attention because she emphasized that at the end of each session, she would help me identify concrete tools I could use to work on myself and to modify the areas of concern I had. My therapist joined me on a journey into self-discovery over the last nine years of my life. While I was working with her, she invited me to experience family constellations—the systemic therapeutic approach mentioned in Part One of this book. She also suggested a six-month workshop about transpersonal psychology, into which I enrolled.

One of the great benefits of attending therapy was to be able to take a guided deep dive into my inner life. Whatever the methodology, my therapists held my hand in the process of throwing light into my dark places. Attending therapy was a space to listen to myself and to validate what I was feeling as something worthy of being named and examined with compassion. My therapy sessions were sacred places, away from the noise of everyday life, where I could disclose my feelings,

71

cry, examine, and reframe my interpretations. By setting some time aside every week or every other week, I was telling myself I was important enough to do this for my wellbeing.

Therapy was also an exercise in humility whereby I consented to ask for help and allowed myself to be questioned about my responsibility in the co-construction of my unhappy life events. I had to be humble enough to realize I was actively collaborating in perpetuating unhealthy behaviors and toxic thinking with some of my attitudes.

In all my therapy sessions, the therapist was a loving mirror who asked the appropriate questions to enable me to see myself with more clarity but also with more compassion. The therapists who worked with me showed a receptive and welcoming energy that helped me feel appreciated and sustained when I was falling apart. They taught me how to hold myself in moments of crisis and to build an internal voice that could guide me through the difficult moments.

Through my years of therapy, I learned to identify and reconfigure toxic thinking patterns, to view myself with more compassion, to be willing to see a broader spectrum of possibilities in life, to act courageously when I had to examine and accept my mistakes, to be patient with my shortfalls, to be more considerate of other people's emotions and internal lives, and to reframe different life dimensions. Session after session, I was able to create a set of tools to guide me when the storms struck.

CARING CONVERSATIONS

In my process of reconnecting with my inner self, conversations with my family and friends were as equally valuable as therapy. Talking to these caring people about my life concerns, aspirations, fears, and happiness helped me process my own thinking and to understand how to create my life journey.

Although my brothers are younger than me, they have forms of wisdom that help me see life and myself in a richer and more insightful way. They have been an amazing mirror in helping me see both my virtues and mistakes. They talk to me with complete honesty and help me remember things about myself I'd sometimes forgotten. They know me better than most other people and I feel I can talk to them about any pressing issue in my life. They make me laugh about my mistakes and encourage me to take life less seriously. My brothers bring to my life an incomparable male perspective, which helps me understand how certain aspects of life look like from another viewpoint.

Conversations with my brothers aren't always easy—sometimes we get defensive with each other; we struggle to be concise or patient, or we simply become too stubborn in our positions. However, I am certain that through our conversations, the three of us have learned to improve our communication abilities. I respect my brothers because they have different life experiences, which are as valuable as mine. Through my interactions with them, I keep learning to be more observant of myself, more empathetic, and grateful with life.

In addition to my brothers, talking to my friends has been an enduring way to find healing and meaningful realizations. I have an amazing group of female and male friends who have come into my life at different, crucial moments. With many of them, I have remained friends for more than a decade. I view each of them as *earth angels* who came to this life to share their life journeys and to support me through mine.

All my closest friends are smart, compassionate, service-oriented, family-oriented, humanist people who care for the world around us. They are also brave people who seek self-growth every day in their lives. Like me, they are imperfect but they understand the value of self-improvement and they work to achieve that diligently. My friends like hearing my stories and they share theirs openly. In this exchange of stories, we have learned to be respectful and also critical. We understand each one of us is open to learn and that our feedback comes from a place of respect and love. We've never had to discuss the agreements or rules of friendship; however, we learned from the first day to value and appreciate each other as intelligent people. We are grateful for our encounter in this life and we are committed to co-create stories together.

In this busy and rapidly changing world, it is a great blessing to have the attentive ears of friends who can open space and time in their busy schedules to hear one's struggles and to offer caring advice or help make sense of the world out there. These days, it is a luxury to be able to rely on trustworthy people who are willing to engage in serious and courageous conversations.

I have enjoyed having female and male friends tremendously. High quality friendship is a blessing. I think it's one of the most loving spaces we can find to learn about life. There is a common assumption or prejudice that suggests men and women cannot be friends because of sexual tensions. I have found this assumption incredibly wrong. I have enjoyed and learned amazing things from my male friends. They have all been caring, tender, and respectful human beings. They have taught me to listen to and learn about the male perspective of life.

My friend Omar deserves special attention. We have co-created so many stories together over the years. He has become like an older brother to me; most importantly, he has been a life master. He is my mentor, colleague, supporter, and unconditional friend. He persuaded me to study abroad and his advice and support transformed my life in ways I never even imagined. At each critical stage of my life, he has been there to listen to me, support me, and encourage me to learn more. He has also opened his heart and shared his personal stories to show me the fragility and complexities a man can experience in the various dimensions and stages of life. He is a brave man and his sense of humor has always been the best remedy in my moments of crisis. He has a huge desire to serve others and to make this world better. He is kind and patient. He is humble to own his mistakes and has a great desire to improve.

I could not have asked for better friends. They are committed to doing things with integrity and to be honest, courageous, and loving. They all have amazing work ethics, discipline, and a desire to serve others. We have honored our friendships as a space for mutual support, healing, attentive listening, and empowerment. We are each other's advocates, cheerleaders, and informal therapists when the need arises. We authentically celebrate each other.

Self-Help and Scholarly Books

As a woman with an active mind and intellectual curiosity, I find pleasure in gaining new knowledge. I am particularly attracted to grasp new concepts and theories as well as the relationships and connections between them. I am equally drawn to academic books as I am to self-help and spiritual books. Many of the books I've read over the years include books written by therapists, spiritual guides, and investigators. I don't discriminate any source of knowledge: Buddhism, Spiritism, positive psychology, sociology, social psychology, cultural psychology, or numerology.

The collection of books I've read throughout my life have shaped my core beliefs. As part of my education and professional work, I have read a vast number of scientific articles and books across many branches of the social sciences. Among my favorites are those from cultural and social psychology, anthropology, and sociology. When I was studying for my doctorate, I realized some of my favorite books were those about Buddhist principles. They helped me learn how to calm my overthinking and rumination. I realized the importance of developing a healthy mental diet by choosing your thoughts rather than letting your mind run wild with toxic chains of ideas. Through those books, I also learned that fear, uncertainty, hope, and love are all a part of life.

Another set of my favorite books included those talking about non-western ways of knowing. I wanted to learn about alternative sources of knowledge that could help me see life beyond the boundaries of rationality. Knowing about the life of my grandfather, Margarito, who had a passion for the psychic world, led me to understand other ways through which I could make sense of life. I read about synchronicity, angels, soul mates, past lives, manifesting one's destiny, numerology, women as psychics, tarot, and dreams. All these types of knowledge sources expanded my perspective about life and provided me with creative ways to see life beyond the traditional frames of reference.

As a scholar working at a higher education institution, I have encountered colleagues and friends who deemed this type of book as lacking sufficient scientific evidence to be considered an authentic source of learning. However, I prefer to think life has more than one way to be seen and interpreted. As a social scientist, I have realized my practice, which includes research, teaching, and mentoring, has become more effective because I give myself permission to think freely—within science and outside of it. I view my rational thinking and world as valid as my magical thinking. Up to this point, my hybrid way of thinking has taken me further in trying to enjoy and make sense of my existence.

SPIRITUALITY

In the realm of the divine, I have found an endless source of hope and trust. I trust in a higher source of energy or intelligence that uses unconditional love and acceptance as a source of expression and manifestation. Of particular relevance is the image of angels. These divine forms of energy are to me as real as the leaves on the trees I see every day.

I grew up in a Catholic family. I was taught to both fear and love God as an omnipresent divinity. My great grandma, Consuelo, was a highly religious person. She not only attended church every day but also lived a life based on ethics, service, empathy, and compassion. She was one of the most forgiving, humble, faithful, humanitarian, and altruistic people I have known. She and my great aunt Isabel were babysitters for my parents during certain parts of my childhood and they instilled a great sense of faith and spirituality into my life. I believe Consuelo was a sort of spiritual guide in my life; she joined me as a child when I needed it most and still does every day, even if I cannot see her next to me anymore.

In addition to my great grandmother, I had an adopted grandmother, Luz Maria, who had taken care of my parents when they were in the orphanage. A single lady who lived close to us and who also babysat for my mom when I was a teenager, Luz Maria (Miss Lucha, as my family used to call her) gave me support and moral guidance through her everyday life lessons. She instilled in me the importance of making critical, reasoned decisions in life, encouraged me to question traditional social practices, and to value faith as a central part of life. She was both an intellectual woman and a committed Catholic. She was very compassionate with an amazing capacity to serve others and to express her love in creative ways. Similar to my great grandmother, Luz Maria was another earth angel in my life.

I view spirituality as a vast field of knowledge and practices that have no other purpose than enhancing our human nature. Central to my understanding of spirituality is the need to engage in the practice of service. I don't see myself as claiming particular membership to a creed of religious association. Instead, I view myself as a person who can honor and value the spirituality of Mexican indigenous people, Catholicism,

Buddhism, and Nature itself. I view spirituality as a practice that invites us to attain higher levels of consciousness through the enactment of unconditional love and respect for and service to others (person, animal, tree, insect, water, or mountain).

I treasure three core components of spirituality: praying, my belief in angels, and service. Prayers represent my capacity to talk to the universe and use language as a way to connect and to recite my energy to the perfect order that governs beyond my present, past, and future. I believe in the power of language as an affirmation of self, the spirit, and the collective consciousness. I pray to sing my faith to the universe. I pray to reaffirm my existence. I pray to communicate the love I profess to those who matter to me and those whom I don't know yet. I pray to invoke energy when I am falling apart. I pray because I create myself through language and conjure my existence through self-affirmations. I pray to call my destiny. I pray to request protection and guidance. I pray to evoke the creative energy and intuitive wisdom connecting us together as one heart.

The way I see it, angels are transcendental beings who watch over human existence to provide guidance, help, and protection when they are invoked. Throughout my life, I have felt their presence and believe I am heard and protected when I talk to them. In the quiet space of my solitude, they are the pillars of my peace of mind.

Finally, orientation toward service has been crucial in the cultivation of my spirituality. I have learned helping others is a way to help myself and vice versa. We are all connected; we are one big, interconnected heart. The success of our brothers and sisters is required for our own individual wellbeing. Central to my understanding of service was my parents' story of their lives in the orphanage, NPH. My story today is in some way possible because of a kind priest, Father William B. Wasson, who decades ago selflessly decided to offer a home and protection to hundreds of children without parents. In that act of compassionate service, I see the amazing series of miracles one man's heart can bring to this world.

PHYSICAL ACTIVITY

While spirituality brought guidance toward connecting to a higher source of energy, exercise helped me connect to my inner body by becoming more aware of my physical skills and endurance capacity. During my doctoral studies, daily physical activity helped me process anxiety and deal with the everyday stress of work. It is no secret exercise enhances one's body in many different ways: it helps to increase energy, fight depression, improve cognitive functions, and release endorphins that help us to feel happy. Exercise also brings a sense of accomplishment.

I wasn't actively involved in sports as a child. I gravitated toward books rather than physically challenging activities. Most of the time, I was afraid of my physical education classes at elementary, junior high, and high school. I wasn't good at playing sports so being under public scrutiny and making mistakes was a big source of anxiety when I was a child and later as a teenager.

Although I never came close to being an athlete, I liked being active and particularly enjoyed dancing and walking. As an adult, I've gravitated toward gym classes where I can combine music, movement, and physical endurance. Walking and going to the gym every day have become an essential part of my routine over the last two decades. Being a woman who can easily spend a large part of my time inside my own thoughts, I know it's important for me to reconnect with my body on a daily basis and to make sure I incorporate movement as part of my agenda.

Exercise has a powerful effect on one's spirit and body. It makes us test the boundaries of our strength, our ability to persist, and our focus. Over the last five years, walking meditations have been one of my preferred forms of exercise. Walking with my dog in my university campus every day, around trees and green grass, is a great privilege and a gift I give to myself. Exercise is a way to honor and show respect to oneself. The way I see it, exercise is an expression of self-care.

WORKSHOPS

Lifelong learning opportunities are important because of three reasons. First, they integrate conceptual knowledge (information from a specific field) that helps us find ways to address specific problems or gaps in our understanding. Second, workshops activate our desire to learn something new and the relevance of being lifelong learners. Third, our desire to participate in workshops starts with a state of humility through which we acknowledge we don't know everything and we can learn from and with others.

Learning is fundamental for personal growth. Embarking on new learning opportunities is a way to say to the universe one is open to expand one's mind and spirit. Through my personal journey, I have found interesting workshops that offered me a chance to learn about better forms of communication with others, about using art as a form of expression, and about transpersonal psychology. Workshops are a great opportunity to come together with other people as we explore our curiosity and desire to learn. Collective learning is the prime venue in the pursuit of self-improvement. Learning together with others is the expression of a collective desire to grow as one shared heart.

PODCASTS

Online video conferences are a contemporary way to use technology as a relatively free tool and self-prescribed strategy to learn—any day, any time. Podcasts epitomize the rich expansion of knowledge across the planet. People from different regions, fields of expertise, and generations share their narratives and ideologies with the world to create knowledge communities.

Podcasts create cross-cultural connections with people interested in what the podcasters have to say. The podcasters are united in their desire to share insights and wisdom; their listeners are united in their desire to hear and learn the insights and wisdom the podcasters have to offer. They are a form of creative expression using technology as its platform.

Podcasts and any other online-based video have become a relatively easy way to access a huge diversity of experts and banks of specialized knowledge. In the last seven years, I've become a persistent listener of podcasts. Listening to various types of podcasts (psychology, politics, sexuality, health, spirituality, motivational, philosophical, or physical training) helped me find creative answers to my never-ending questions. Podcasts are a highly practical means to gaining valuable pieces of wisdom in a rapidly moving world. Now more than ever, we are experiencing a world where knowledge expands at an incredible speed; through podcasts, we have the privilege to find different approaches and experts who can provide us with insight to make sense of our life concerns.

The eight creative projects I've described above have been essential to helping me use different forms of knowledge to improve myself. I must emphasize, support and collaboration are at the core of all these creative projects. It is the connection and interaction that we establish with others, whether familiar or unknown, that is critical to igniting our personal growth. It is crucial to acknowledge personal development cannot occur in isolation; we need others to learn about ourselves, to reach higher levels of awareness, and to develop new skills.

Personal growth is an interconnected process; when we share with others what we have learned, we are helping them grow as well. Therefore, personal development is ultimately a collective endeavor and we can all collaborate in each other's progress. Without the practice of writing, taking therapy, talking to friends and family, exercising, reading self-help and scholarly books, attending workshops, listening to podcasters, and learning from spiritual guides, I would have not been able to achieve the realizations I have today.

The construction and maintenance of relationships was crucial to navigate each one of the three pathways I followed, and to develop and maintain each of the eight creative projects in which I engaged. In every social encounter lies the seed of individual enlightenment. Coming together is the opportunity to realize what we are blind to see when we are by ourselves.

10

ABOUT DOGS AND CATS: LITTLE ANGELS WITHOUT WINGS

When I look back at the aspects of my life that helped me understand myself at a deeper level, I realized pets have played a unique role.

Pets hold a very special place in the development of human life. Men and women find in their pets a way to express love, care, and solidarity. I have always thought animals come into our lives to help us learn and grow as social and spiritual beings. Having to take care of a dog or a cat (or any other type of pet) forces us to be less self-centered, more patient, observant, disciplined, and to express our emotions. In our modern world, in which being busy and alone are becoming common conditions, pets have become loyal companions in our daily lives.

In my personal experience, having a dog allowed me to express my caring side. It also allowed me to see some of my shortfalls. For some of my friends who are also successful professionals, having a dog or cat is an integral part of their lives; it helps them explore their maternal or paternal instincts. Pets give us the opportunity to create forms of attachment that enable us to experience both life and death as we see our furry friends come into and depart from our lives. Our dogs and cats teach us about the joy of life and the pain of loss. They make us strong with every day they are with us, and even stronger when they say goodbye.

I have owned pets since I was 15 years old. The dog I have with me today, Ted, came to my life in 2011. He was a gift from my mom. She gave him to me as a way to cheer me up after I came back to Mexico from the United States, following completion of my doctoral studies. After six years of living independently in the United States, I experienced a major reverse culture shock, which caused some depression. Ted became my God-sent gift. He helped me recover my smile by paying attention to his tiny and cute existence. I forgot about my pains and struggles by making sure he was safe and sound every step of the way. He became a loyal companion.

Prior to Ted, I had five dachshund dogs: Jackson, Jackie, Pili, Layla, and Jack. Each one of them was a miracle in my life. We shared many adventures together and they made my teenage years joyful with their presence. I hugged them when I felt lonely, talked to them when I had words burning in my chest, and played with them when I was happy. They passed away in time, and while their departure brought tears to my face, they also left countless loving memories in my heart. As a teenager, my dogs helped me to be disciplined, careful, compassionate, and empathetic. Taking care of my dogs made me understand my wants and needs were not the only important matter in the world and I had to think about the needs of those around me, like my pets.

Ted, my small white poodle, is nine years old. He is not a perfect dog; similar to me, he had his own process of self-improvement to conquer. Ted was prematurely separated from his pack, which caused a unique set of attributes in the construction of his dog personality. Ted likes being the boss and having things done his way. He is an anxious dog that struggles to relax, causing him to be very jumpy and easily scared. He doesn't like to walk in the dark; he doesn't trust the unknown world of the shadows. He likes silence and peaceful spaces; he can be overwhelmed when things are out of routine or when new people come into his space. He loves walking with me and joining me as much as possible, wherever I am. He doesn't like walking around crowded stores and begs me to pick him up when surrounded by strangers. Unfortunately, Ted's anxiety manifests as aggression sometimes.

Ted and I have many things to learn together and a lot of his issues mirror some of the areas within myself that I need to improve as well. In that sense, Ted seems to be part of my life to help me address those areas of my personality.

Ted's bossiness and stubborn disobedience reminds me I have to be confident and I can use my voice to command authority in the room without hesitation. His anxiety reminds me I need to learn to be relaxed and to nurture my internal peace. His fears remind me I have the capacity to be protective and to trust my strength when facing challenges and difficulties. Ted's dependency reminds me I can learn to let go. He also helps me express my tender and maternal side.

Ted reminds me I can be playful and that life is not always about being serious. Every day, he forces me to stand up, leave the computer, and play with him. Every day, when we are driving back home after our morning and afternoon walks, he stares at me for a little while, as if he is saying, "Thanks, mom, for taking the time to walk with me outside." His cute eyes tell me I should not forget the beauty of the natural world.

Ted is a constant reminder of my mom's love and a reminder of the beauty of nature. He is my personal piece of heaven, my fluffy little white cloud. Ted's presence in my life also lets me see the loving patience of my family and friends, who have showed tolerance for and consideration of the challenging personality of my four-legged, furry friend.

Every one of my dogs have been a blessing in my life. They have been my opportunity to give back to Mother Nature, my reminder for improvement, and my opportunity to practice love and patience. Our pets are an extension of us and they represent an opportunity to grow and learn about ourselves. Our dogs and cats are eager to help us learn and grow; it only takes our attentive and caring gaze to understand the messages hidden in the depth of their lovely, grateful eyes.

PART II: SUMMARY

Throughout this part of the book, I have shared the story of how I was able to reconnect with my inner self. It has shown my journey from the acknowledgment of my dark places to the identification of strategies and ways I can use to reach an improved and empowered *me*.

Self-development is a creative endeavor because we create new versions of ourselves with each new experience and learning we acquire. The process of becoming anew is possible because of the creative energy (love) that ignites our actions and the intuitive wisdom that gives them direction. In our daily lives, we tend to forget creativity is a human capacity that is not exclusive to the likes of painters and sculptors. We are all creative because we have the innate capacity to create our being and journeys as we move from one place to another, from one minute to another. We are creative beings not because we do beautiful, artistic things but because we have the capacity to author our lives with the good, bad, and ugly actions that shape our personal trajectories.

Authoring ourselves is, without a doubt, one of the most creative expressions we can produce. We write our lives, little by little, through the decisions we make—as well as those we avoid making. Our actions and the lack of them are acts of creation. Authoring our lives happens whether we are entirely aware of it or not. However, becoming critically aware of the actions we choose to author our lives can make a difference between being active or passive creators of our lives.

An active creator of life holds ownership and power over the journey she or he is authoring. A passive creator relinquishes power to external voices and mandates; he or she allows others to make the choices. The first actively *leads* a life; the second passively *accepts* a life. The first views him- or herself as an actor with power and agency; the second views her- or himself as powerless or a victim of events and people. Critically aware creators acknowledge that within them reside the power and imagination to create a good life, in spite of the challenges. The uncritically passive creator lacks understanding of their ability to tap into their internal power and imagination to improve themselves.

Realizing one's creative energy is a crucial step that takes us from being passive reproducers to conscious creators of ourselves and the world in which we live. Many aspects of the social world depend on our capacity to reproduce certain things like language, rules, and institutions. Without reproducing certain social aspects, we wouldn't have a language to communicate with one another across multiple generations; we wouldn't have social rules to guide behavior. Without reproducing certain aspects of social life, we wouldn't have social institutions like schools or hospitals that help us organize collective life and collective needs.

However, reproduction is not enough to exist and grow as a society; our evolution and progress as humanity also depends on our creative capacities to think in original and innovative ways. Therefore, being creative is beneficial not only for the individual person but also for the collective self. Being aware of and using our creative energy enables us to move into a place of higher self-understanding and appreciation. The expression of our creative energy becomes evident through the small and large projects we choose to pursue: our jobs, the families we create and sustain, the pets we take care of, the hobbies we engage in, the stories we tell to others, the stories we tell to ourselves, and the plants and flowers we grow.

Creation is both a simple action and a complex collection of practices. It is both a small victory and a lifetime accomplishment; it lives in solitude and in collective work; it is both abstraction and flesh, and is expressed in silence and the uproarious voice. Our creative energy is both an innate force and an educated talent; it is who we are and who we can become.

Creation will never be an individual event. We create with others, for others, and because of others. We all collaborate in the marvelous construction of ourselves and the world we live in. Acknowledging the unique creative talents each one of us possesses will help us understand how we can collaborate with others in this inspired design we call life.

PART 3

Co-created Stories: The Love That Connects Us

NOTES FROM A HUMMINGBIRD

We come together to co-create love stories made of the creative energy we put into the world; every connection we make is an opportunity to learn and to grow.

In this part of the book, I want to share with you some of my learnings about engaging in romantic relationships. My goal is to open a dialog in how men and women can be more sensitive and reflective about co-creating relationships with one another. Most of the following chapters will focus on the ways in which I have navigated romantic relationships. However, I also want to emphasize the value of female-male interactions *beyond* romantic interests.

Non-romantic relationships between men and women offer amazing opportunities for growth and mutual support when we open ourselves to the possibility of learning from each other while respecting and valuing our sex/gender differences. It is my perception that we tend to overlook the value and importance platonic female-male relationships have in the construction of our lives. Men and women can build healthy, respectful, and productive relationships that do not have to be romantic in nature.

Both feminine and masculine energies are important to construct a complementary life. Welcoming both types of energies and learning how to manage them as we author our lives is essential to reach personal fulfillment. Neurosciences have documented the differences between the female and male brains. Each type of brain has unique strengths and forms to perceive and engage with life. There is value in learning about how men and women can bring their unique ways of perceiving and doing to create conversations and relationships.

From my position as a heterosexual woman, I have spent a substantial part of my life trying to understand how men and women can learn together about giving and receiving love in more compassionate ways. The desire to find a loving partner is probably one of the aspects of life we worry about the most. We aim to find someone with whom we can share our life and experience joy. Novels, movies, poems, TV shows, sculptures, and other artistic expressions have been created to celebrate and glorify the quest for the one and only true romantic love.

In spite of the hopeful scenes we see and hear again and again in love stories and fairy tales, many of us experience love and relationships from a less than ideal place that often involves tears, pain, frustration, or insecurity. Many of us have not been properly guided or educated to experience romantic love from a healthier place where personal erasure or collapse is not required to find a loving partner. These coming chapters trace my journey into a healthier place in which I don't have to experience solitude or terminated relationships with weakening pain.

The stories I will share with you depict two processes I underwent during my interactions with men:

Firstly, my struggle to see my personal value when trying to connect with them. Often, when we enter a relationship without a clear understanding of our personal value, we are prone to engage in toxic styles of attachment.

Secondly, my effort to reconnect with myself and re-affirm my personal value in the romantic relationships I chose to engage in. Entering a romantic experience with greater self-awareness and confidence can lead toward healthier styles of attachment.

Through these two processes, I realized it was essential to learn to see and value myself as much as I see and value the man I am interested in. I realized the value of being assertive. I understood I wouldn't create a healthy connection with someone without being entirely aware that my existence and personal attributes were as equally valuable as those of the man I was attracted to. I had to learn that loving someone did not mean loving myself less or erasing myself.

In the pages that follow, I will share the realizations I gained from my relationships with the men I dated. As I share my experiences, I hope you can find points of correlation between my journey and yours. It is my wish that my experience may be a mirror to help you learn a bit more about yourself. Most importantly, I hope that as you read these chapters, you may find wisdom with which to create healthier interactions and relationships with the men who cross your life's path.

11

UNLEARNING: PRINCE CHARMING AND THE FAIRY TALE

We live in a society in which most of us are love illiterate. We struggle to understand what love is, how it should be expressed or received, and how to grow through love. The formal curriculum at most schools is not particularly designed to teach us about love or relationships in a humanistic way. Additionally, families don't always operate with enough awareness to teach their members how to build healthy love relationships.

Most of us learn about love informally, accidentally, and experientially. For many of us, Hollywood movies, songs, and fairy tales have become a common point of reference when we try to make sense of our incipient love experiences as teenagers or even adults. As we grow older and develop more sophisticated ways of making sense of life, our perspectives may change. However, it will usually take some serious heartbreak before we are redefined as more mature and wiser lovers and lovable persons.

My story may be similar to yours. I entered my teenage years expecting to find Prince Charming and build a fairy-tale like relationship in which everything would automatically fall into perfect place. I had a very simplified and idealized understanding of what romantic love and human relationships were supposed to be about. I had no understanding of gender dynamics, family stories, styles of attachments, personal perceptions, cultural stereotypes, or communicative interactions. My awakening to romantic love was tougher than I imagined and it would take me several years to heal from bad dating experiences and re-build my understanding about love. I had to unlearn the simplified versions I had heard and seen in popular culture.

For me, unlearning popular understandings of romantic love started with making sense of rejection as a natural experience rather than a threat to my sense of identity. We rarely stop to think and make sense of the dynamics of rejection and acceptance as we venture the cold waters of dating and romance. This becomes particularly damaging when we have a debilitated sense of identity, which many of us have when we experiment with love as teenagers. Sadly, many of those initial love experiences create scars that permeate our later forms of interactions.

Romantic movies, songs, and fairy tales rarely portray healthy ways to interpret rejection or "failure" when it comes to loving someone else. During an important period of time in my romantic life, both rejection and indifference from guys was internalized as personal failure, which increased my insecurity and marked my forms of interaction with them.

From my teenage years to my middle 20s, I perceived myself as being unsuccessful in attracting guys. I would become interested in a guy who didn't reciprocate my feelings because of unknown reasons. I often assumed the reason for their indifference was tied to my personality. I was not a popular girl or an extrovert; I didn't engage in risky behaviors, or make an obvious display of my sexuality (by way of makeup, short skirts, colored nails, etc.). I saw myself more as an introvert, a compliant and committed student with family responsibilities that more often than not forced me to act older than my age.

Most of the time, boys my age approached me to make fun of my serious demeanor or what they perceived to be my hyper commitment to school. I felt very inadequate around guys all through my school years, including graduate school. My closest experience to having a boyfriend occurred toward the end of my doctoral studies, during my mid-20s, when I started dating my first "boyfriend," who we will call Romeo # 1.

During most of my teenage years and young adulthood, I felt a great failure when it came to attracting a guy. I didn't see myself as an attractive girl. My self-esteem issues made it incredibly difficult for me to feel worthy of love and to be confident enough to display or express my personal attributes. I struggled to feel comfortable in my own skin. The anxiety and fear of rejection made it easier to hide my life behind my schoolwork and family obligations. I didn't know how to approach guys, to engage in conversations, or to be flirtatious. The stress of being rejected or mocked made it very difficult for me to put myself out there in the dating scene.

With each unsuccessful attempt to attract a guy, I started to feel more and more anxious, frustrated, hopeless, and inse-cure. I was afraid of becoming an unlovable woman destined to be alone for the rest of my life. While the perceptions of my romantic life—or lack thereof—were exaggerated, they seemed real to me at the time. I allowed my narrow interpretations of life to persuade me there was something wrong with me and that I would never be good at attracting the opposite sex. With years passing by and me being single, Prince Charming and the fairy tale seemed to become less and less attainable. My anxiety around my love life increased. I envied the romantic success of many of my female friends, whom I viewed as possessing everything I lacked.

In hindsight, I realize my early experiences with romantic love were characterized by a misrepresentation of my ability to interact with guys or to be appreciated by them. With limited guidance as to how to navigate an incipient romantic life, I internalized a negative self-image. I started to assume I was not enough and if a man did pay attention to me, I would have to overextend myself to convince him I was worthy of his attention and love. I misconstrued the love equation; I assumed that to receive, I had to give more than the other person. In this inaccurate mathematical interpretation of love reciprocity, I learned to love too much, to settle for receiving less, and to develop an anxious form of attachment[8] in which I was constantly worried about being abandoned.

My anxious attachment meant I needed constant reassurance of love or attention from the other person. Founded on an incessant fear of not being enough, this attachment style caused me to interpret any small act of indifference as a threat of abandonment. The possibility of being left alone was scary and therefore something to be avoided or prevented in any way possible.

My anxiety and fear of abandonment led me to overextend myself, to tolerate acts of indifference and disrespect, and to not voice my needs because I was afraid of being perceived as needy, clingy, or irrational. My anxious attachment style permeated the two longest romantic relationships I had (3 years and 2 years) and some of the brief dating experiences I had after that.

Therapy and reading books around human relationships were critical creative projects that helped me identify the ways in which I was entering the world of love. I realized the preconceived notions I had about love and relationships, along with my debilitated self-image and low self-esteem. Through therapy, critical self-reflection, and self-initiated learning, I understood the importance to let go of Prince Charming and the fairy tale. Instead I started to develop a more realistic and complex understanding of what human relationships mean in the field of romance. I learned to name my fears (abandonment, loneliness, rejection) and to see myself with more compassion and self-love.

In the last couple of years, I have learned to enter new romantic experiences from a place of greater awareness, self-love, and self-respect. While it is fair to say I have experienced some setbacks, I have learned more about men and myself. The quest for new realizations has not been painless; with every new date there is the chance of another heartbreak. However, learning to give and receive love can only occur when we are willing to be vulnerable and co-create experiences with someone else.

Unlearning simplified versions of romantic love brought new realizations. First, it helped me understand the romantic journey is not about finding Prince Charming; it is not about him. The primary responsibility is to find ourselves: our voice, value, needs, shortfalls, and areas of growth. Without confidence and a clear direction of who *we* are, we won't be able to make the right choice or see the other person clearly for who *they* are. With a debilitated self and a wounded self-perception, we allow anything and anyone to come closer because the fear of rejection or abandonment is greater than the need for self-respect.

The second realization was about letting go of the fairy tale to embrace the complexity of real-world romantic relationships. Romantic love is not a given; it is not magically, spontaneously, and easily constructed. It requires both personal and collaborative work in the form of increased self-awareness, compromise, commitment, flexibility, adaptability, openness of mind, compassion, forgiveness, tolerance, patience, and continual learning. Real love stories start with two people realizing a sense of shared responsibility to create a story of resilient love. Through each romantic relationship, either long or short, there exists the possibility for the participants to rewrite themselves and to write new and better stories together.

12

TOXIC CONNECTIONS: FROM GOD-LIKE FIGURE TO MY OTHER HALF TO THE ENEMY

In this chapter and the next, I will discuss both toxic and healthier ways of connecting to a romantic partner. While these chapters will not cover all the types of toxicity that can arise when building a romantic relationship, I will focus on one critical aspect: the place in which we position ourselves when we enter a romantic relationship.

We can enter a relationship either being aware of who we are and our value, or erasing ourselves and forgetting our value. In the first scenario, we are closer to creating something healthier because we come together with someone else being aware of what we can offer and what we can demand from a place of respect. In the second scenario, we are at risk of creating a toxic relationship because we silence our wants and needs while pouring ourselves into serving and pleasing the wants and needs of someone else, even if they didn't ask us to do that.

As I described before, during my teenage years and 20s, I developed a distorted perception of my position in relation to guys. When it came to thinking about them as romantic partners, it was all about them: who they were, what they wanted, what they expected, and what they found attractive. I overlooked myself, my needs and desires, and I became overly concerned with fulfilling their expectations, or more precisely, my interpretation of their expectations. My attention was focused on them entirely and I forgot to see myself in the co-creation of a love story.

Later, I would learn I also built an asymmetry into the way in which I perceived the value of them as opposed to the value of myself as an object of love. I saw them, the guys I was attracted to, as icons of perfection. I struggled to see them in their right proportion as normal human beings. Instead, I perceived them as flawless, superior, more attractive, and more valuable than me. In my mind, I was smaller than or inferior to them. Unconsciously, I put every guy I was attracted to on a high pedestal. Thus, trying to reach any of them felt very intimidating and difficult to achieve.

Secretly, there was a constant fear of never being enough to catch the attention of the god-like figure I was falling for. With such distorted perceptions, it was very daunting and kind of hopeless to be chosen by any of the objects of my admiration. This way of thinking of and perceiving them was rooted in a strong lack of self-esteem and low confidence. Seeing them as superior to me made it very difficult for me to approach or talk to them, to act naturally or confidently around them. I felt inadequate when I was in their presence, uncomfortable, and worried they would see all my imperfections at first glance.

My perception of them as god-like figures derived from my belief that I had many shortfalls. Simultaneously, I failed to see them as imperfect human beings. This misinterpretation was reinforced by my lack of success in previous romantic endeavors. The less effective I was in attracting someone's attention, the less confident I became in matters of the heart.

Parallel to this sensation, I started to believe that to be truly happy and visible, I needed to be chosen by a man. I didn't want to be the non-chosen one. Nurtured by countless cultural icons, imageries, and messages, I thought a man had to come into my life and rescue me from my loneliness, incompleteness, emptiness, and imperfection.

I was looking for my other half and as long as I was single, I felt incomplete. I felt I needed a man to legitimize my existence. I had the distorted perception that my value as a person would only become tangible once my Prince Charming would come to rescue me from social anonymity, boredom, and my own self-depreciation.

Wallowing in the depths of this distorted perception, I failed to acknowledge my attributes, value, personal and professional successes. What I didn't understand at the time was my tendency to exalt men as perfect set me up for failure because I was making it impossible for me to reach them. The more I perceived myself as inferior to them, the less likely it was for me to approach them and give them a chance to get to know who I was. The vicious cycle in which I trapped myself made it very difficult for me to develop a romantic relationship with any man, simply because I wasn't giving myself or them the chance to learn and appreciate who I was.

During this time of my life, one of my biggest issues had to do with my capacity to see myself as a beautiful woman. Since my childhood, I've struggled to embrace my physical appearance. Some insensitive comments delivered within my own family and some bullying experiences at school planted the seeds of low self-esteem. Somehow, I allowed those negative experiences to affect my perception about my value as a girl and then as a woman. Sadly, I started to believe it would be very unlikely any guy would find me attractive. Therefore, when Romeo # 1—a handsome, intelligent, dark-skinned, Indian guy—agreed to go on a date with me, I felt I had to do anything in my capacity to persuade him to stay with me, to choose *me*.

Romeo # 1 and I were the same age. He was the lead singer of a rock band and a smart guy who was finishing his undergraduate studies while I was finishing my doctoral degree. When we started to date and he brought me to his house to meet his parents, I felt I was the luckiest woman alive because this handsome guy had picked me—for the first time. At the age of 26, I finally had my first "boyfriend" and my first kiss. He became my god-like figure and my other half. In the light of his seeming greatness, I overlooked and forgave any act of disrespect, indifference, and avoidance from him.

Over a period of three years, I lived in denial about his inability to consistently commit to a relationship with me. He selectively defined our relationship as one of "friends with benefits" according to his convenience. In spite of my discomfort, I muted my desires, my needs, my anger, and my requests because I didn't want to upset him for fear he would leave.

Thus, in my relationship with Romeo # 1, I erased myself as a way to preserve a less-than-ideal relationship. My fears and low self-esteem made the ambiguity of the relationship we both built acceptable. I lied to myself, pretending I was okay with being halfway accepted and halfway denied. I gave my silent consent to those terms, even when they were hurtful. I allowed it because I didn't want to be alone and because at the time, I felt I needed a guy to validate me as a woman.

In spite of all the shortfalls, my relationship with Romeo # 1 helped me feel I was capable of attracting a guy. It helped me believe I wasn't destined to be alone forever; it gave me hope. However, with the chance of being seen and chosen came the fear of being abandoned. For as long as the relationship lasted, I held onto it as hard as I could. I felt my sense of identity and happiness depended on it.

My desire to make this relationship last led me to do one of the most emotionally costly things: to annihilate myself in an attempt to preserve my connection with someone else. I developed an anxious attachment to him; I worried about when he would call me and when I would see him; I wondered if he still liked me, or if he would meet someone prettier or smarter or more adventurous than me. It was all extremely stressful as I tried to sustain and nurture this ambiguous relationship, especially during the period of time it was long distance (we were two countries apart), while trying to hide my anxiety and insecurities.

Eventually, the relationship ended. I decided to stop making the effort to meet and stay with someone who was not certain of his desire to be with me. During this breakup process, therapy work was crucial to help me bring my sight back to myself; it helped me gather the courage to remove myself from an unhealthy situation. The breakup crushed my heart, tore me apart, and sunk me into depression. With a debilitated self, I felt that without him, my value was gone again. Gradually, therapy and all my other creative projects helped me reconstruct myself. With many emotional scars still needing healing, I entered a period of singlehood lasting a couple of years.

Being single and frustrated about the challenge of connecting romantically, I became resentful toward men. I resented their lack of interest in someone like me. I was frustrated because in spite of my effort to improve myself, I felt no man seemed to care about what I had to offer. I struggled to understand what men wanted in a woman. I became discouraged as I watched some of my friends find the wishes of their hearts (at least from my perspective) while I remained with my loneliness.

Among my single friends, criticizing men became common practice as part of the girl talk. Talking about men's shortfalls was our coping mechanism to conceal our pain and to escape part of our responsibility in addressing the issue. It was easier to perpetuate a discourse portraying men as immature, insensitive, or inadequate than talk about our deepest fears and insecurities. In an effort to avoid an authentic self-analysis, men became the enemy. Labeling men in that way (as the enemy) enabled us to escape confronting some of our own shortfalls or to simplify love and relationships.

Seeing men as god-like figures—as the other (better) half—and as enemies came from a place of anxiety and fear: anxiety to find someone who would make me feel valuable, someone to overcome my fear of remaining alone forever, and someone to help me prove to the world I was worthy and attractive enough to be chosen. For as long as I held this perspective about men, I felt being single was the equivalent of having a scarlet letter that said I was the unwanted, the non-chosen woman in a world where couples are celebrated and where being in a relationship is seen as the pinnacle of a fulfilled life.

Time and renovated wisdom would show me my desperate craving for a romantic relationship concealed a sense of discomfort with myself. After years of not taking care of or attending to the relationship with myself, I finally came to a point in my life that pushed me to practice self-love and self-acceptance *before* trying to fall in love with a romantic partner again. The journey I would begin included a renewed understanding of myself and heathier ways to interact with men. I slowly started to rebuild my self-perception and my perceptions about men.

13

HEALTHIER CONNECTIONS: FROM IMPERFECT HUMANS TO LIFE MASTERS

My romantic life during this third decade of my life has been characterized by a more conscious effort to move toward healthier ways of interacting with men. This change in perspective was not spontaneous; rather, it has resulted from a desire to overcome my fears, rebuild my self-esteem, and address my anxious attachment style.

This period of my life has not been without bumps or setbacks but it has been a stage in which I've achieved improved self-affirmation. My engagement in the eight creative projects I described in Chapter 9 (writing, therapy, conversations, scholarly and self-help books, workshops, spirituality, exercise, and podcasts) have played a critical part in my move toward healthier behaviors and interactions with men. All the learning endeavors associated with each one of those projects helped me understand my personal value and appreciate the various roles I play in my everyday life. I became aware that my identity is not limited to being either single or a man's girlfriend. I had to acknowledge my life was made up of many other accomplishments, factors, and elements: I am a productive professional, an immigrant, an artist, a writer, a committed daughter, a supportive friend and sister.

As I won a few of the battles against my low self-esteem, I started to shake off some of my fears and insecurities. Not everything went away; some scars of my misperceptions remain. However, I am now more mindful about the moments when my mind engages in toxic ideation. I learned to identify my mind's unhealthy habits and choose to reframe my thinking more consciously. I also started to recover my personal voice and to express what I did and didn't want in a relationship without being afraid of losing the man or making him mad.

This healthier way of building a romantic relationship was slowly and persistently constructed in the midst of a new stage in my life as a professional and a daughter. After I finished my doctoral degree and postdoctoral work in California, I returned to Mexico in 2011 where I worked as an assistant professor for four years. I always intended to come back to the United States, so I kept looking for job opportunities there. In 2015, an opportunity arose and I was fortunate enough to be hired as a university professor in a public state university in California. In this new place, I found an ideal context within which I could continue pursuing my calling as an educator. This change—coming to a new country and leaving my family behind once again—was another major transition in my life. It forced me to reconfigure myself as a person and a professional. I was both excited and terrified about starting my life again in a foreign country.

I arrived at my new place with only two suitcases and a big desire to conquer the unknown. Although I had lived in the State of California before, the cultural differences between Southern California and the Central Valley were marked. In addition to that shock, I had to learn about my new job, the geography of the place, new regulations, as well as the values and challenges of the community.

In spite of the excitement of obtaining my heart's wish (a new job in the United States), my first semester wasn't easy. The new experience was emotionally demanding and a solitary process. As with previous times in my life, destiny put earth angels along my way. From my arrival to this day, my friend and colleague, Shellie, became my earth angel, mentor, supporter, counselor, and official cheerleader. From day one in my job, she was committed to help me enrich all areas of my life.

Six months after I started my job in this new city, I met a guy at a public event. I had gone to the event as a way to become involved with the community and start developing new networks. At the end of the event, I approached him and introduced myself. He was welcoming and we engaged in a conversation lasting for almost an hour. During this initial conversation, he eloquently recounted part of his life journey. I was captivated by his presence and intrigued by him.

During the weeks after our first encounter, things unfolded in a positive way for both of us. We started dating and, different from my experience with Romeo # 1, he proudly welcomed me into his life as his girlfriend. We developed a committed relationship that lasted two years.

My Romeo # 2 was a kind and clever guy. He had a European heritage and he proudly expressed his masculine side by being protective of me and helping me resolve everyday problems. He also had a feminine side, evident in his talkative style and his tender way of caring for his plants and for others. Different from me, he was an extrovert and confident enough to strike up a conversation with anybody, anywhere. He encouraged me and helped me to integrate into the community and familiarize myself with the region. He introduced me to his family and friends. He loved studying history and I enjoyed listening to his accounts about worldwide, national, and historical events. Talking to him was never boring; we always found things to laugh about together. We had oppositional paradigms when making sense of social life;

nevertheless, we managed to respect each other beyond our ideological mismatch.

My relationship with Romeo # 2 was not perfect. Even though we were compatible in many ways, the timing wasn't right. After two years of being in a relationship, we realized we needed to continue our separate ways. He said being in a relationship was not a priority for him. While hearing his decision was very painful, I had to acknowledge it was the right moment to end the relationship.

As opposed to my relationship with Romeo # 1, this time I wasn't willing to stay in a relationship where I was neither entirely embraced nor valued as a romantic partner. This time, I wanted to believe in my value and not feel afraid of being by myself again. With this healthier understanding of myself, we were able to go our separate ways. We agreed to remain friends and with that last conversation, my mourning process began. Going through all the stages of grief lasted several months. This breakup process brought both pain and substantial growth.

Romantic breakups can be emotionally devastating. Part of our reality gets torn when we cannot find complicity in creating a shared romantic journey. Anyone who has experienced a heartbreak knows the pain that can flood the spirit and the weakening sensation a departure brings. For me, the breakup triggered two interconnected processes. On the one hand, I had to figure out how to overcome the pain of loss and feel joyful again. On the other hand, I had to learn to be at peace with my solitude and to rethink my ways of relating to men.

Being alone again brought back fears, self-doubt, and insecurity. It was hard to recover my daily routines and everyday spaces without the person I had fallen in love with. Crying and missing our time together was a daily occurrence. I had to re-learn to be with myself and to conquer my surroundings again.

For a while, it was difficult to see beyond the pain and find peace and mental clarity. I went over and over the memories of the relationship, trying to find logical justifications to the end of the story. The more time I spent caught up in a cyclical revision of my story with him, the less time I had to appreciate the opportunities for growth that existed if I dared to embrace the transition. I realized authentic healing could only occur if I was open to see the hidden lessons that existed beyond the pain. I learned there is a difference between seeing a breakup as a definite ending rather than a transition or an opportunity for renovation. In a definite ending it seems as though there's nothing left to build. However, in a transition there is opportunity for creating new beginnings and to become someone different as well. When I dared to reframe my pain into an opportunity to grow, the authentic healing started to occur.

Reframing the pain involved taking a step outside the sadness to examine the development of the romantic relationship with Romeo # 2, and myself as an active part in it. My change in perspective started with a decision to stop seeing him as an enemy and feeding my negative assumptions about him. When things ended, I felt sad and frustrated. I felt Romeo # 2's lack of desire to continue in the relationship with me was selfish and immature. When my anger cooled, however, and I took time to observe and make sense of some parts of Romeo # 2's life, I realized my negative interpretations of his response toward our relationship was an oversimplification of him as a person and his personal journey. I had to be able to appreciate the complexity and challenges he was going through as part of his personal pathway.

When I opened my eyes and mind to see him as a person who—like me—also experienced problems, dilemmas, and challenges, it became possible to interpret his decision with less resentment and more compassion. I started to understand his inability to build a romantic story and a shared life path with me didn't come from a place of malice. I realized the breakup wasn't only hurtful and painful for me but for him as well. In one of our conversations, he cried as he asked me to forgive him, and I realized he was also struggling to end our relationship.

In the realization that our timing was off, he was suffering as much as I was. I understood our life journeys were out of sync; we were moving at different paces and our life goals were different. We were at different mental and emotional stages in life and we couldn't force the co-creation of a romantic story anymore. We realized we had to honor each other's life journey and needs. We worked to re-signify our relationship and come together as friends who could learn to support one another.

Beyond the pain the breakup brought, I found reaffirmation of my value as a person and the courage to re-inhabit my solitude. In the midst of this renewed inner strength, I was also able to see him with more accuracy and compassion. I realized a broken relationship wasn't a conspiracy to hurt me.

At the end of the story, I saw two broken hearts rather than only one (mine). I was able to acknowledge two people (him and me) trying to figure things out and overcome life's challenges. In this awakening, I challenged my perception of him as an enemy and started to see Romeo # 2 as an imperfect man who, like me, was trying to learn how to love in the midst of personal shortfalls and dilemmas.

When I shifted my perspective, new possibilities of interpretation emerged and I saw my romantic relationship as an opportunity to learn and grow personally. He, and any man before and after him, became a life master. I chose to believe Romeo # 2 had come into my life to help me understand more about love, myself, and life. With the opportunity to find a learning lesson in my romantic encounter with him, I reframed the breakup as a transition into a new form of awareness and growth.

With this change in perspective, I discovered I was able to navigate pain with more grace and hope. For me, the breakup became a chance for self-actualization and the possibility to create a different story. I realized not all the stories I was able to co-author with a man were meant to be romantic or long-lasting; some were short-lived and destined to be stories about friendship or ephemeral coincidences.

Several months after the breakup with Romeo # 2, I actively looked for opportunities to go on new dates. Whether through online dating or fortuitous events, I ventured out to explore the dating landscape again. Some of the connections that were built lasted one day, one week, or a couple of months. At the beginning, every unsuccessful date revived the pain and some of the toxic thoughts and emotions. However, I continued to try and I realized that with each new experience I learned more and more about myself, solitude, life, and society as a whole. Little by little, I added strength to my inner voice and my hope.

During this dating process, I continued to be engaged in my various creative projects (artistic expressions, going to therapy, caring conversations, reading self-help books, participating in workshops, engaging in spirituality, doing exercise, listening to podcasts). Each one of those projects was critical to my reconstruction. The learning I derived from these projects helped me address my insecurities and fears as well as recalibrate my misperceptions.

The dating experience turned into a parade of short and long stories of *me* and *them*—some of them worthy to be turned into a comedy/drama television show. In the co-authoring of these stories, I learned I still had self-work to do. I saw my growth but also the areas still requiring improvement. Each man with whom I had the opportunity to connect offered me a reflection of who I was and how I was projecting myself to the world. Dating became a space for the creation of shared stories and the recreation of souls. I realized that at the end of each encounter, however long it was, I came out with new learnings.

Some of the men I met were willing to engage in a process of self-discovery and share their insights with me. Others were more silent. As I continued to date, I witnessed the infinite kindness of some men. The resiliency, integrity, caring, and keen presence of one man in particular, Roberto M., continues to amaze me. He epitomizes the continual search for self-improvement, resilient love, and desire to build healthy connections with a woman. We met six years ago and while our story was not meant to be one of romantic co-creation at that time (due to geographical challenges), we both implicitly agreed to co-create a story of support, companionship, mutual respect, and admiration. Even though we live far away from each other, we decided to create a story of friendship that still exists today. We share our dilemmas, stories of growth, successful events, and even pain with one another.

The dating world allowed me to understand more about men and myself. Even when I wasn't able to co-create the desired love story with some of these men, we co-created stories of romantic resiliency. These were stories of people who value meaningful connections and who wanted to believe in the possibility of finding a partner in spite of the personal dilemmas and challenges of everyday life. Through these stories, I realized men can be caring, trustworthy, honest, compassionate, and supportive if I was able to see beyond their imperfect actions or words.

With each new date, I purposefully focused on discovering the qualities of each one of them and the prospects for learning they could bring into my life, even if they didn't stay with me. I learned to trust the process and let life amaze me with opportunities to welcome other souls crossing my path.

14

THE CONTINUUM OF GROWTH:
LESSONS LEARNED

Re-entering the dating world after a relatively stable relationship can be scary, intimidating, and demanding because one has to be willing to show vulnerability and to express emotions, life expectations, and insecurities. Dating can be emotionally draining when meeting a new person doesn't turn out the way we expect it to. If we aren't emotionally strong or mature, a series of unsuccessful dates can strip us of our confidence and hope.

However, searching for that *significant someone* isn't a solely negative experience; it also brings excitement, hope, illusions, and fun. Meeting new people generates unique possibilities to learn about oneself, to refine social abilities, improve communication skills, and discover other people's stories and trajectories. Dating can be a creative adventure and a stimulating opportunity to discover multiple dimensions of life.

It wasn't until my mid 30s that I was more intentional about trying to meet new people. As many people do, I jumped into the dating experience with limited understanding of myself and, what's more, I was quite clueless that was the case. I also had limited experience in expressing and assessing emotional maturity once the interaction with a new person started.

Consequently, the date parade was a mix of good, bad, and ugly experiences. I came face-to-face with some of my own shortfalls, and I also met guys who were clueless about what they wanted and how to express emotional intimacy without feeling they were compromising their masculinity.

One day, after a series of unsuccessful dates that reopened some old wounds, I decided I was tired of feeling defeated after every date that didn't work out. I knew I needed to find a way to continue dating without feeling my emotional stability would be compromised every time a new encounter didn't have a successful outcome. After examining the story of each date, a lot of personal reflection, and my usual engagement with the creative projects to improve myself, I realized I had to reframe the way in which I was engaging in new dates. Rather than entering each new encounter with fear, anxiety, or hesitation, I needed to change the energy I brought when meeting a new guy. I had to bring joy, confidence, peace of mind, and conviction that my strength would be sufficient to confront the uncertainty innate in the dating process.

Entering each new romantic opportunity with a desire to learn and grow helped me move from a place of fear and frustration to a place of higher awareness and self-love. I changed my mindset: I chose to believe no matter the final outcome of any date, I would find something useful and joyful to learn about myself and life in each opportunity to come together with someone new. Although my quest to find a partner has been less than perfect, it has challenged me to be more patient and to reach greater self-acceptance and comfort with my solitude. I learned my ability to create healthy bonds with a guy resides in my capacity to love and respect myself a bit more every day.

When I examine each one of the romantic experiences and stories I have co-authored, I can trace a process of growth and more thoughtful decisions. I have realized jumping into dating can be an amazingly fruitful opportunity when one comes closer to another person with the deliberate desire to achieve personal development. Dating doesn't happen *to* us; instead, it happens *for* us. We can choose how to approach, frame, and step outside the dating process. We don't have to be victims of romance; we can be agents of our own romantic stories. We have not only the ability but also the responsibility to dictate how we can begin and end each new romantic story.

My interactions with each man helped me grow in ways I couldn't have done by myself. While all the social relationships we build in our life (with parents, friends, mentors, colleagues, community, etc.) are sources of growth, romantic relationships have a unique way of enabling emotional maturity, adaptability, and self-discovery. The intimacy and erotic nature that romantic relationships bring with them touch our lives in both subtle and significant ways. Romantic partners have the capacity to strum the strings of our souls, to enter the labyrinths of our mind, to dig deep into our hearts, and to echo permanently on the layers of our skin.

Each man who came into my life was a key ingredient in my recipe of self-growth. I realized many of these men saw me with much more kindness and compassion than I saw myself. I started to understand each man chooses and decides his definition of beauty. I learned I had to stop imposing my own definition of beauty upon them. I realized beauty is a negotiated and contextualized event defined by two people rather than a fixed set of attributes dictated by one of them.

With this new understanding, I reconciled with my physical appearance and my personality. I learned to see my beauty again. I learned I could be a sensual woman because of my mind, body, and soul. I realized I could be less demanding with myself and less self-critical. I learned to be less anxious about my level of efficiency when interacting or communicating with men. I allowed myself to make mistakes, to have patience, and to learn from those less than perfect circumstances. I learned to feel comfortable with my imperfections.

During my dating journey, I learned to be less focused on my pain and to be aware that men are also fighting their own internal battles and dilemmas. I discovered men also struggle to gain confidence or to feel accepted. They look for acceptance and are afraid of rejection. In spite of the cultural narratives that portray men as emotionally detached, invincible, and unbreakable, I've heard men talking about their fear of heartbreak and their tendencies to create walls and isolate themselves as a way to avoid pain. I came to understand they find it difficult to name and manage their emotions in clear and healthy ways because they, like many women, have not been guided to make sense of and manage anger, anxiety, fear, insecurity, and pain.

I understood men crave to express their thoughts and emotions without being judged or perceived as less masculine. I learned to relinquish my prejudice about men being heartless, indifferent, and selfish. When I started to be less defensive and less anxious about my own concerns, some of the men started to feel more willing and comfortable to express their emotions. The more I was able to identify and process my own emotions, the better able I was to handle deeper conversations with them and listen to their emotional struggle as well.

Some of the men I met brought a kind of masculine energy to my life that helped me relax and be receptive rather than reactive. For some moments, I was able to stop excessively relying on my masculine energy (rationalization, problem solving orientation, leading approach). I reconnected with my feminine self, which allowed me to embrace the receptive and nurturing nature that defines my womanhood. They reminded me I could ask for help and that I could welcome a compliment or kind attention.

I comprehended that if a date, or series of dates, didn't turn out in the ideal way I expected, incompatibility was not a sign of my personal failure but rather the result of two life stories moving at a different pace. I understood the successful creation of a romantic story didn't depend on my solo authorship but on the miraculous synchrony of otherwise randomly ordered intentions, moments, and concerted events. I learned to listen to and trust my inner strength and my internal voice. I came to appreciate that beyond the unfulfilled romantic expectations, there was an opportunity to learn and to grow. I was able to take responsibility for my toxic areas and to look actively for ways to detoxify my thinking and actions. Further, I was able to engage in self-criticism without destroying myself through perfectionism.

As I moved from one date to another, I learned to differentiate between a healthy internal voice and toxic thinking. My healthy internal voice came from a place of self-acceptance and compassion while my toxic, perfectionist rumination stemmed from a place of fear and unhealed pain. My healthy internal voice encouraged me to express love (creative energy) and act through it (creative expression), and guided me to expand love by co-authoring creative connections, which inspired self-growth for those who participated in them.

Throughout my dating journey, I am grateful to have found my reflection in the mirrors each relationship made available for me. It is my hope that as I searched for self-construction and for a partner, I was able to inspire or bring growth opportunities for the men in my life as well.

15

RESILIENT LOVE: COMPASSIONATE DATING IN THE CONTEMPORARY WORLD

Throughout my own romantic stories and those I've heard from my female and male friends, I see the strength of resilient hearts. In spite of the challenges and the heartbreak, many of us are willing to keep trying and hoping for the possibility to build healthy romantic relationships.

In today's challenging world, I am optimistic about the construction of resilient love. This type of love is made of faith, personal empowerment, commitment to growth, effort to overcome everyday challenges, desire to procreate life, increased mutual acceptance, and an unapologetic intention to search for joy and personal fulfillment.

As I write this book, our world is undergoing a severe social crisis triggered by an outbreak of a pandemic disease (COVID-19). This financial and public health crisis has forced us to redefine our everyday routines, to practice social distancing, and to rely on technology as the primary means of sustaining our most meaningful relationships and work lives. It is within this unique experience that we still try to defy the odds and come closer to one another.

Over the last ten years of my life, I have realized that the possibility to co-create a successful romantic story goes beyond the desire of two people to get together. Rather, it resides in the artful navigation of everyday demands and personal insecurities. In today's world, compassionate dating seems a desirable approach to get to know someone and co-create romantic stories. I view compassionate dating as a disposition characterized by a desire to understand each other's stories. In this type of encounter, there is a conscious effort to be empathetic, to express vulnerability, and to show respect for the life and emotions of the other person.

Being able to engage in compassionate dating requires us to learn how to connect and communicate in the midst of the distracting noises and challenges of the inside and outside world. The modern world—our context for dating—is a tapestry of multifaceted events: technological innovation, massive knowledge dissemination, economic crises, political distrust, immigration issues, environmental deterioration, gender tensions, racial tensions, health emergencies, and so on. While we witness accelerated social change and material innovation, individuals' adaptability and awareness to engage in self-development and healthy relationships seem to barely keep up with the speed of change.

Part of the reason why the level of sophistication of our inner lives and relationships is not comparable to technological innovation may be related to the limited attention that we, as a society, pay to our socio-emotional development and psychological wellbeing in the midst of our fast-moving lives. Throughout our personal journeys, many of us rarely receive expert support to learn how to successfully engage in a process of self-construction and non-violent, emotionally mature, and healthy relationships with members of the opposite (or same) sex. It is in this plethora of challenging conditions that men and women try to coincide and co-create shared stories.

The complexity of our modern world seems to create competing agendas for many of us: serving the individual self (for example, career advancement and success) or serving a collective purpose (for example, building a family). In the field of romantic relationships, this dilemma translates as a constant tug-of-war between seeking attachment and preserving autonomy. Through my dating experiences, I found some men seem to perceive a sort of opposition between the pursuit of personal projects and the construction of shared lives. Consequently, even though people are looking for connection they also feel threatened by the possibility of long-term commitment or the investment of time to know a significant other.

Attachment, which is the foundation for human survival (hunters and tribes protected and helped each other to thrive and survive), is now perceived by some people as oppositional to an autonomous existence. Previous negative romantic experiences can bring a sense of skepticism, hesitation, or fear of being attached again. However, it's important to realize attachment doesn't mean sacrificing one's existence, voice, and desires to the will of someone else. Attachment is not the antithesis of autonomy but rather its heightened expression. Attachment relies on the successful construction of an autonomous life that welcomes the possibility of complementarity. We can learn how to develop healthy forms of attachment (as opposed to co-dependency) in which a loving partner can enrich our personal projects rather than threaten them. We can learn to come together without losing ourselves.

In addition to overcoming the dilemma of attachment versus autonomy, we can learn how to make technology an ally rather than a hazard to our mental health or relationships. Technology has not only provided us with infinite ways to improve our lives but it can also increase the levels of stress when we use it indiscriminately. While technology has brought unimagined ways to make distance fade away and processes shorter, the use of smartphones and computers has brought new challenges and disruptions to our traditional ways of interacting.

The increased use of social media has influenced the construction of relationships and forms of communication among individuals. At times, we may feel tempted to replace hugs with tweets or likes, face-to-face encounters with video calls and endless texts, and genuine caresses for sexting. Be assured, I'm not attempting to demonize technology but to identify how we can use it so that our social and emotional lives are enriched rather than disturbed. The outbreak of a pandemic disease in the atypical year of 2020 forced us to redefine our relationships through the use of technology; we are yet to assess the impact of an elongated period of heavier reliance on virtual encounters and connections on humankind.

The question that alludes us is how we can use technology as a way to strengthen our inner lives and to bring us together rather than create tensions for us. The COVID-19 experience has shown us technology is a pragmatic and even elegant solution for many of our needs; however, it cannot substitute face-to-face interactions or compensate our personal insecurities, fears, internal struggles, or unsolved dilemmas. Engaging in a critically aware use of technology includes personal responsibility and care.

In addition to developing critically aware uses of technology, we can also redefine our culture around the use of time and prioritization of demands. The imbalance between attention to work and other areas of life can create isolated and overworked people. When the pursuit of productivity and success is compulsively practiced (workaholism), some practices such as self care or the search for a significant other can be perceived as a distraction or a waste of time. Being chronically busy can leave limited or no time to pay attention to our wellbeing and to build meaningful relationships.

When we take time to analyze retrospectively the stories of the emotional bonds we have created, we will notice our most valued relationships were not built during a 30-minute chat. High quality relationships demand an investment of time. In a society that prioritizes productivity and financial success, many people may think that investing time for relationship-crafting is a luxury they are not able to afford anymore. In a context in which our commitment to work will continue to be a priority, we need to be mindful of the importance of taking time to build meaningful connections with others. Giving ourselves the opportunity to look for a special someone should not be seen as a waste of time but the healthy expression of our need to connect.

Another aspect of our culture that is characterized by certain degrees of confusion among men and women is the enactment of gender roles in current times. Prior to the 21st Century, Western societies operated more markedly under traditional gender expectations that located men as rulers at the top of the social structure, while women occupied more submissive and service-oriented roles.[9] Public life was primarily seen as the domain of males whereas private life (domestic roles) was perceived as the domain of women. With the expansion of postindustrial societies and the incorporation of women in the job market, women and men's roles in society had to be adjusted. Nowadays, in the midst of the social changes we are experiencing, men and women are still learning how to redefine gender stereotypes and change gender practices.

With the current debates about female empowerment and toxic masculinities, many of us feel somewhat confused about how contemporary men and women are expected to participate in the initiation and development of romantic relationships. Women are encouraged to adopt more masculine traits (e.g., engaging in leadership) and men are expected to integrate more feminine qualities into their attitudes and behaviors (e.g., being more emotionally expressive).

These new social expectations have made it challenging to readjust our ways of interaction with the opposite sex. Women, once told to affirm themselves and conquer the public sphere, risk being judged as individuals trying to castrate men. Men, once told to be more emotional and communicative, may be judged as effeminate when they express their feelings or decide to become a stay-at-home dad. Some professional women, like me, may feel disoriented about how to embrace their success and approach men without making them feel emasculated. Men may also feel confused about how to treat a woman in a way that shows chivalry and confidence while at the same time validating her autonomy and success.

In addition to the confusions around expected gender roles, there exists a collective sense of distrust between men and women: women condemning and expressing anger toward men for their oppressive history, and men resenting and judging women for their desire to supersede them in positions of authority. Sometimes, we seem to be investing more time competing against each other than respecting our unique virtues and learning how to complement each other. Both the sense of confusion and the distrust characterizing gender relationships in our society can make it complex for men and women to come together.

16

THE BRIDGES WE CAN BUILD: LEARNING TO COME CLOSER

In a complex world that poses multiple challenges for men and women to connect, it becomes crucial to create bridges to find and meet each other. We can learn to reestablish trust, communication, and respect between us. Reciprocal support and mutual growth are possible when we choose to see our counterparts with heightened consciousness and humility.

Based on my retrospective observation of the meaningful relationships I was able to build with the important men of my life, below I describe four relational bridges that can help us come close to one another.

Let's Learn about Each Other

Many of us have a knowledge gap about how it is to experience and make sense of life from the perspective of the opposite sex. Each one of us relies exclusively on the unique understandings of our own bodies, personal stories, mindsets, desires, and expectations. From my experience as a heterosexual woman, neurological and socio-cultural differences lead men and women to experience the world in different ways. Hormones, brain structure and functionality, skills, cultural understandings, and life stories give men and women different and distinctive possibilities of expression and styles of affirmation in this world. Neither is superior to the other; they are complementary. In the desire to learn more about each other, listen to each other, and value each other resides the opportunity for men and women to build healthier and more compassionate relationships.

Some years ago, I read a few books about the neuroscience behind female and male brains.[10] Beyond the debates of the scientific validity or political correctness of talking about the differences between female and male brains, for me it was extremely enlightening to read these books. They helped me understand a lot about the ways in which women and men process the world as well as the unique traits and skills that each sex possesses.

As I read these books, many of my experiences with men and women started to make more sense. I was able to learn more about my own biological condition as a woman and the ways in which my brain has unique and amazing ways of shaping some of my behaviors, attitudes, and emotions. They also helped me to better understand, appreciate, and respect the male brain.

While there may be many contextual factors that can moderate neurological functions and hormonal effects in the behaviors of men and women, each sex has remarkable abilities with which to understand and navigate this world. Nowadays, learning about manhood and womanhood, femininity and masculinity has become increasingly accessible. In addition to the physiology behind the female and male brains, there is a great number of gender studies that can help us understand the social and cultural experiences of men and women in society. Women can benefit from learning more about who men are and the struggles they have also experienced. Similarly, men can enrich their understanding about who women are and the ways in which their inimitable biological and socio-cultural experiences have shaped them historically.

If we want to help each other grow, to be part of each other's lives, and to better communicate our needs to each other, we should care to learn more deeply about ourselves and about our sex counterparts. Accomplishing mutual understanding is possible, desirable, and helpful toward constructing more compassionate romantic relationships. Nowadays we have easier access to sources of information that are both formal and free, such as e-books, podcasts, and conferences about gender and sex differences.

LET'S BUILD BRAVE SPACES RATHER THAN ASSUMING OR IMPOSING

Arguments, serious talks, or fights with a romantic partner (or a potential one) are often fertile soil for misunderstandings, wrong argumentations, communication gaps, or even aggressive assertions. Either during or after taking part in an emotionally charged conversation with someone, many of us try to find explanations behind what our significant others did or said as part of the critical discussion. We fall into the habit of trying to guess and assume the intentions or motivations behind the other person's spoken words. However, experience has shown me that engaging in that habit can be both conflictive and unproductive. Jumping to inaccurate conclusions, imposing our personal bias, or forcing certain assumptions as ways to make sense of the other person can be a costly mistake.

None of us can fully grasp the meaning of somebody else's words, actions, or intentions without having an authentic two-way conversation that can help us understand who the other person is, what his or her motivations are, and what their ideological perspective consists of. Elusive guessing can be detrimental to any relationship because it doesn't help participants in the relationship to understand each other authentically.

No matter how much effort one puts in to explain somebody else's motives and actions, without the input of the person whom we're trying to understand, we risk oversimplifying or misunderstanding them. Rather than assuming or imposing our bias as part of our effort to make sense of the other person, we should be willing to engage in brave conversations with them. Brave conversations with our significant others should be based on at least three conditions: willingness to be vulnerable, a disposition to be self-critical, and a desire to listen to the other attentively.

Being vulnerable can start with acknowledging and communicating our personal emotions and needs to our significant others. We can help our partners to understand who we are, our way of thinking, and what we need when we openly share our inner lives.

Being self-critical involves the ability to observe and reflect on our own thoughts, intentions, emotions, and actions. The critical assessment of who we are is crucial to realizing our shortfalls and areas for improvement. Engaging in self-critical reflection along with our partners can be understood as an act of humility through which we understand we are not perfect and space for personal growth is possible.

Finally, attentive listening emphasizes the need to defer judgement so as to give our full attention to the other person's words and provide appropriate cues that show empathy, interest, and engagement.

Having such brave conversations with our significant others can be challenging because one has to dare to overcome insecurities and fear to be authentic and assertive. However, the creation of a space within which we can have brave conversations gives us the opportunity to accomplish shared growth and the creative co-authoring of an authentic love story.

LET'S BE LESS SELF-CENTERED AND MORE EMPATHETIC

Throughout my journey, I have realized that many times we become extremely entangled in our own minds—thinking about our own insecurities, unfulfilled expectations, fears, needs, and pain. We sometimes overlook the fact that the individuals we fall in love with also have an internal world they need to decipher and manage.

Probably one of the most important lessons I gained after some dates and relationships is that everyone comes to a new relationship with emotional scars and traumas. Our stories are made of the moments when our hearts were broken and then mended again. Consequently, our scars are not only the memory of our struggles but also a testament to our resiliency. When we come close to someone else to co-create a romantic story, we need to be aware that at the moment of the encounter, each person is at a different stage in their personal journey toward reaching healing, self-knowledge, and emotional maturity. Therefore, we need to learn where each one of us is and identify if there is an opportunity to continue a journey of shared personal growth together or not.

If two people are at very dissimilar journey stages ("bad timing"), then it's important to be respectful of the other person's stage in life and to accept the need to let go of romantic expectations. It is meritorious if, every time we approach a new relationship, we make a concerted effort to learn about the stories and journey of the people we pursue romantically.

Becoming more compassionate toward one another in our romantic relationships involves making an effort to understand each other's struggles and scars. Each one of us has a unique story and part of our homework is to take the time to identify not only *our* stories but also those of the people we choose to love.

Romantic co-creation must start with a personal desire to understand our own journey; however, it is sustained by our desire to learn about the other person as much as we dare to discover ourselves.

LET'S NOT GET FIXATED ON CULTURAL SIMPLIFICATIONS

We live in a society where quick and simplified messages are abundant in our daily lives. We have become increasingly exposed to a multitude of unfiltered images and messages as a result of advertising and social media. With the prevalent use of smartphones, we are easily bombarded by information, marketing, politics, debates, and advocacy groups. In an interconnected world where information and online communication must move at an incredibly fast speed, we sometimes don't take time to reflect deeply on specific ideas, or to question social tendencies or stereotypes.

The uncritical reproduction of traditional practices or belief systems can cause the construction of unexamined or unintentional lives. One of the traditional practices entrenched in the collective consciousness is the tendency to see those different from us as threatening or inferior to us. However, every time we automatically judge another person as less than us, we deny ourselves the opportunity to learn something about them and so expand our social awareness. If we can embrace the idea that each person who comes into our lives embodies a lesson we can learn through them, then we can establish a different type of connection with them. When we enter a new relationship with a desire to learn from the other, our possibilities of co-creating romantic stories will expand.

I invite you to join me in *not* oversimplifying those who are different from us. Instead, let's give ourselves the opportunity to listen to their stories and learn where they come from. Overcoming cultural simplification requires us to take some time to learn who the other person is. It consists of moving beyond gender stereotypes and macro narratives that dictate rigid roles. It involves a creative effort to decide who we are and who we can become together. Overcoming cultural simplification involves moving beyond practices in which people treat each other insensitively or as disposable, simply because we are too quick to judge and take too long to listen.

PART III: SUMMARY

Throughout this part of the book, I've shared some of my romantic stories and the ways in which I learned to reflect on and reframe my interaction with men. Critical to this section is the idea that our desire to look for a romantic relationship is an opportunity to accomplish two crucial things.

First, each romantic encounter or connection—whether it lasts one hour, one week, a month or a year—is an opportunity to learn about ourselves and our forms of attachment. We can learn about what it means to be a man or a woman in the dating world. We can use our romantic encounters to learn about our personal stories and the stories of the people we date.

Second, entering a romantic encounter gives us the opportunity to engage in deliberate co-creation. Participants in the dating world come together with the opportunity to use their creative energy to co-create a shared story whose episodes can be negotiated or determined by them. Not all romantic encounters finish in a romantic relationship; however, all romantic encounters can engage in co-creation. The two people who come together with the idea of exploring romantic expectations may find there is no chemistry or spark between them; they are at incompatible life stages or have incompatible goals. In spite of their differences and the mismatch, these two people *can* co-create something together: an intellectually stimulating conversation, a series of funny conversations, an enjoyable trip, a relaxing walk, or even a friendship that can last for as long as they both decide.

Compassionate dating is possible when the two people who come to an encounter to explore romantic expectations are open to learn from one another and are willing to participate in a process of co-creation. That process of co-creation can take any shape or color, but it must bring a sense of contentment and joy for the people taking part.

Two people can come to a date with the explicit agreement to do their best to co-create an enjoyable moment. Through my experience, I realized that entering a date with a mindset open to co-creation will guarantee greater joy and less frustration. The lack of compatibility of two people in the romantic realm does not mean they cannot build something significant (e.g., friendships, collaborations, projects) if the conditions allow it.

The quality of the relationships we can co-create with others is connected to the quality of energy we put into the world we live in. The possibility to co-create resilient, compassionate, and authentic love stories resides in our ability to not only see *ourselves* with care but also to take the time to learn compassionately about who the other person is. Learning about our own personal stories and learning about the stories of the partners we choose to love is an essential step toward co-authoring a shared life in this increasingly challenging world.

FINAL WORDS

17

HUMMINGBIRDS IN MY HEART: HONORING THE STORIES OF MY JOURNEY

My life journey, like yours, is made of a composite of intertwined stories. Some of those stories belong to anonymous people who passed through my life quickly and silently. Other stories belong to significant people who came into my life for short or long periods of time. As part of my personal journey, I co-authored learning experiences with people who became important to me and who helped me grow and understand myself better.

On these last pages, I want to honor the presence of those people in my life whose stories have enriched my journey. We crossed each other's pathways and in so doing we co-created an instant, a story, and the world we live in. Thank you for being a master and helping me to grow. Your presence in my life has been relevant and appreciated. You have created part of the person I am today.

My extended family—Mama Chelito; my godparents, Consuelo and Arturo; Roberto and Ana; my aunt, Isabel; and Miss Lucha—have co-authored countless stories of love and commitment with me. Grandparents, you were gone long before I opened my eyes and yet I feel you present in the stories my parents told me about you. The stories of each one of you have taught me about resiliency, altruism, service, faith, and respect. The stories of familism we have built together show the strength of our Mexican culture, the courage of our hearts, and the creativity of our hands to give to others and to show kindness to the world.

We have co-created ourselves persistently, unapologetically, and intentionally. That is our message to others. As a big family, we carry the pain and joy of those before us; their births and their deaths gave us life. In gratitude I honor your life stories. The stories of my intergenerational family are the roots of my passion and the echo of my heartbeat. There is no story without them, and with them any story is possible.

My story is also a co-creation with my friends. You entered into my life one day and you decided to stay with me and to let me witness the stories of your life. You have showed me your pain, your glories, your patience, your admiration, and your greatness. You share with me the challenges this world presents. We fight side by side to make sense of the world we inhabit and do something good in return. All of you have listened to my stories multiple times, with patience, providing insight, and helping me to see myself in moments of blindness. You made me feel valued, asking my advice, and expressing your gratitude. You have healed me through your love and by accepting my love too.

I value each one of the stories you represent because you are resilient in times when it's not easy to live every day with a passionate heart. You have cried with me, and our shared tears have made me feel I'm not alone with my pains and my struggles. You have also smiled with me and reminded me that life is good. We are witnessing this world together—its magnitude, cynicism, and possibility for renovation. You are believers like me, and your ideals keep igniting this miracle we call life. My story is colored by your presence; you make each episode brighter. My story is the story of *us* and *we* are the story of our world.

The story of my calling is a unique one, made of teachers I have never met but whose works I've read again and again. It is also made of the stories of professionalism and devotion I've witnessed in my colleagues and supervisors. First in Mexico and now in the United States, I see your work and you inspire me to learn more and to do better. I have been lucky to learn with you and from you. I am certain your spirits work every day to heal this world and to awaken people's consciousness.

In the stories we write together, we advocate for authentic learning and human development among the people we work with. I celebrate with you the stories of success among the students we guide. We keep trying to understand the complexities of the world we live in and we dare to change it, step by step. We work to be co-authors of change and to re-write our existence. The stories we write together are stories of hope and of faith in a society where everyone's stories matter to us.

My life is also a co-creation with nature. Beautiful earth, you have given us your green mountains and trees, your mesmerizing sky with planets, satellites, and stars, your restless sea, and your tenacious soil. You gave us your creatures to admire, to sustain ourselves, and to choose as our companions. You have nurtured our bodies and our spirits by giving us everyday miracles in the form of rain, a rainbow, or an eclipse. I have sustained this life with the gifts you give us; I cannot write any story without you sustaining me with water and air. You have taught me the importance of being resilient when disasters strike. You gave me a chance to live through the perfectly designed encounter of an egg and sperm. In the eyes of my dogs, I see your kindness and I feel grateful when a piece of you looks back at me with gratitude.

My story with you, nature, is a story of perpetual admiration and respect; it is also a story of grief because of the ways in which we take resources and life from you. My story with you is a story of gratitude toward your splendor, and a story of pain when I realize the harm we do as we create our story as a modern civilization.

My place here today is also the story of a country that believes in transnational collaboration. Mexico is a country that—like many other countries—exhibits both glory and deep scars. We are made of blood, hope, and passion. Above everything, I see in my country a story of collective resilience, strong family ties, creative survival, warm friendship, glorious indigenous knowledge, and clever humor. We are a place where colors, landscapes, and stories blossom every day. We are a welcoming soil that opens our forests, gardens, archeological zones, deserts, mountains, and secrets for the curious eyes willing to discover who we are.

My story is shaped by my country's support to study abroad. I am here today because my country believes in the valuable knowledge and expertise other nations can offer to the world. While we are a country that struggles in multiple ways, it is the strength of its people that inspires me to keep going. In authoring my story, I thrive to be a responsible ambassador of the spirit of good, hardworking, family-oriented, disciplined, smart Mexican people who aspire to make this world a better one.

Mexico, you vibrate in my heart and you walk with me each step of my way. I miss you every day. In the Mexican immigrants I see in America, I keep finding inspirational stories that remind me of the value and pride of the stories we create as a nation, as a community, and as leaders.

My story with you, my dear reader, is the story of human search for personal realization and transformation. As you walk with me through the last lines of this book, I hope you realize you have co-created this story with me. You are here with me because you share my desire to make this a better world, a place that can be inhabited by people who are willing to dive deep into their inner selves and learn more about who they are.

As the end of this journey is in sight, I want to thank you for taking the time to learn about my story. Most importantly, I thank you for giving yourself the opportunity to start exploring and making sense of your own story as you learn to discover yourself. I wish that throughout these pages, you found opportunities to identify with more than one of my stories. I also hope you found resources and insights to support you as you continue to author your life story.

I believe that in reading my story you can discover more about yourself.

I believe my story is a part of your story too, and our story is one of continual and shared growth.

ENDNOTES

1. The following is a foundational book to start exploring the notion of narrative therapy: David Denborough, *Retelling the Stories of Our Lives: Everyday Narrative Therapy to Draw Inspiration and Transform Experience,* Kindle Edition (W. W. Norton & Company, 2014)

2. For a deeper understanding of *Casa Hogar Nuestros Pequeños Hermanos* (NPH), you can visit their website and learn more about the story of the orphanage's creation and its current operation: https://www.nph.org

3. The increase of mental health issues in the United States has been explored through different reports, including the following:

    i. Hellebuyck, M., Halpern, M., Nguyen, T., & Fritze, D. (2019), *The State of Mental Health in America.* Retrieved from: http://www.mentalhealthamerica.net/

    ii. The National Alliance on Mental Illness (NAMI) (2018) Retrieved from: https://www.nami.org/About-NAMI/Publications-Reports

4. In the following article, you can learn about the narratives of professional women who feel divided between sustaining both their personal and professional lives:

    Montero-Hernandez, V., Lopez-Arines, E., Garcia-Caballero, M. *Self-castigated Perception and Distress among Female*

Academics in a Mexican Public State University. Review of Higher Education, 42(4), (2019) 425–456

5. For more detailed information about family constellations and the author of this therapeutic approach, the following website can offer critical information:

    Hellinger Schule. Retrieved from: https://www.hellinger.com/en/bert-hellinger-the-original/bert-hellinger/short-biography/

6. For an initial revision of the notion of parentification, the following article may be of interest:

    Engelhardt, J. A. *The Developmental Implications of Parentification: Effects on Childhood Attachment.* Graduate Student Journal of Psychology, 14, (2012) 45–52

7. This book is a great reference to learn about the depth and meaning of mother-daughter relationships:

    Nancy, F., *My Mother/My Self: A Daughters' Search for Identity* (Delta, 20th Anniversary Ed. Edition, 1997)

8. In the field of psychology, the study of adults' attachment styles is an important area of exploration. For a useful book on this topic, review the following title:

    Amir Levine, M.D. and Rachel S. F. Heller, M.A., *Attached. The New Science of Adult Attachment and How It Can Help You Find—and Keep—Love* (Penguin Random House LLC, 2011)

9. To gain a better understanding of the issue of gender inequality and the female experience, the following references can be a starting point:

    Burke, R. J., *Work stress and women's health: Occupational status effects.* Journal of Business Ethics, 37(1), (2002) 91–102

144

Cameron, D., *Performing gender identity: Young men's talk and the construction of heterosexual masculinity*. In A. Jaworski & N. Coupland (Eds.), *The Discourse Reader* (1999) (pp. 419–432). New York: Routledge

Rowland-Serdar, B., & Schwartz-Shea, P., *Empowering women: Self, autonomy, and responsibility*. The Western Political Quarterly, 44(3), (1991). 605–624

Villarreal, A., & Yu, W.-h., *Economic globalization and women's employment: The case of manufacturing in Mexico*. American Sociological Review, 72(3), (2007) 365–389

10. Three interesting books that address the study of the female and male brains are:

Lisa Mosconi, PhD, *The XX Brain: The Groundbreaking Science Empowering Women to Maximize Cognitive Health and Prevent Alzheimer's Disease* (Penguin Random House LLC, 2020)

Louann Brizendine, M.D., *The Female Brain* (Harmony, 2007)

Louann Brizendine, M.D., *The Male Brain: A Breakthrough Understanding of How Men and Boys Think* (Harmony, 2011)

ABOUT THE AUTHOR

Virginia Montero Hernandez was born in Mexico, where she grew up and attained her undergraduate education. She views herself as a bicultural, bilingual person who appreciates peoples' ability to enter and exit multiple cultural worlds.

A university professor, Virginia has lived in the United States for more than a decade. Her experience as an international doctoral student and international faculty has equipped her to make sense of the processes of cultural adaptation, personal growth, and self-awareness.

As a professor and educational researcher, Virginia has devoted her work to understanding the process of identity formation and the value and power of personal narratives to understand people's meanings and life journeys. She has authored and co-authored several articles, book chapters, and a book on higher education.

Virginia works with educational leaders who seek to empower themselves and revitalize their communities. She also explores the ways in which organizations can capitalize on their members' life stories to promote efficiency and success.

In this book, *Chasing Hummingbirds*, Virginia blends her personal and professional voice to explain the process of personal transformation through the identification and analysis of personal narratives.

To learn more about ways to empower yourself and to download a free version of the chart that can guide you to curiously gaze your own life story, visit Virginia's website:

www.creativeselfdesign.com

Made in the USA
Las Vegas, NV
09 November 2021